THE BANISHED PRINCE

Time, Memory, and Ritual
in the Late Plays of Eugene O'Neill

Theater and Dramatic Studies, No. 54

Oscar C. Brockett, Series Editor

Professor of Drama and Holder of the
Z. T. Scott Family Chair in Drama
The University of Texas at Austin

Other Titles in This Series

THE BANISHED PRINCE

Time, Memory, and Ritual
in the Late Plays of Eugene O'Neill

by
Laurin Porter

U·M·I Research Press

Ann Arbor / London

Produced and distributed by
UMI Research Press
an imprint of
University Microfilms Inc.
Ann Arbor, Michigan 48106

Library of Congress Cataloging in Publication Data

Porter, Laurin R., 1945-
  The banished prince : time, memory, and ritual in the late plays
of Eugene O'Neill / by Laurin R. Porter.
  p. cm—(Theater and dramatic studies ; no. 54)
  Bibliography: p.
  Includes index.
  ISBN 0-8357-1934-0 (alk. paper)
  1. O'Neill, Eugene, 1888-1953—Criticism and interpretation.
I. Title. II. Title: Time, memory, and ritual in the late plays of
Eugene O'Neill. III. Series.
PS3529.N5Z775   1988
812'.52—dc19   88-20820
                                                        CIP

British Library CIP data is available.

*This book is dedicated
with love
to my husband, Tom,
and to the memory of my father,
Helmuth John Reininga,
who died on August 9, 1986*

Contents

Acknowledgments

In the many years that I have spent writing this book I have received much help and support, which I would like to acknowledge here. To Michael Manheim of the University of Toledo, Jordan Y. Miller of the University of Rhode Island, James A. Robinson of the University of Maryland, and Frederick Wilkins of Suffolk University go my heartfelt thanks for thoughtful readings of my manuscript at various stages, invaluable suggestions for revision, and generous and much-appreciated encouragement.

To my husband, Thomas E. Porter, my gratitude goes without saying. For his untiring and perceptive readings of endless drafts, his critical acumen and penetrating insights in conceptual matters, and his unfailing love and support throughout this long journey, I feel truly blessed.

LAURIN PORTER

1

Time, Memory, and Ritual

In chapter 6 of *The Great Gatsby,* two-thirds of the way through the novel, Nick Carroway finally learns the truth about Gatsby's past. The flashy millionaire from West Egg, Long Island, it turns out, actually began his life as James Gatz, the son of a poor North Dakota couple:

> His parents were shiftless and unsuccessful farm people—his imagination had never really accepted them as his parents at all. The truth was that Jay Gatsby . . . sprang from his Platonic conception of himself. He was a son of God—a phrase which, if it means anything, means just that—and he must be about His Father's business, the service of a vast, vulgar, meretricious beauty. So he invented just the sort of Jay Gatsby that a seventeen-year-old boy would be likely to invent, and to this conception he was faithful to the end.[1]

Fitzgerald's novel, which paints with brilliant strokes the portrait of the Jazz Age, also touches upon an ineffable longing of the culture at large. As Americans, we feel we should, at any point, be able to begin life over again, to reinvent ourselves. It is an impulse that goes as far back as the Puritans of Plymouth Plantation, who felt that their mandate was to reestablish God's kingdom on earth, to cut themselves off from the corruption of the Old World and start afresh on the green breast of the New. The names by which this enterprise was called—the New Canaan, the New Jerusalem, the City on the Hill—reverberate with religious intensity precisely because the Pilgrims saw it as the last chance God would offer to mankind. Theirs was a divine mission.

By the eighteenth century, although the fervor of the original settlers had shifted from theology to patriotism, the desire to redefine oneself was still evident in the individual as well as the culture at large. It informed Ben Franklin's list of virtues in the *Autobiography,* for example, as he optimistically set out to perfect himself (a list that is mirrored in the "General Resolves" of young Jimmy Gatz, written on the flyleaf of a *Hopalong Cassidy* book), just as it shaped the promise held forth by the frontier as a place to start life over.

The catch, of course, is the unavoidable reality of the past, which precludes the possibility of sailing off unencumbered into the future. Hester Prynne learns that she cannot escape her past by discarding the scarlet letter; she must resume her burden again because it is part of her identity. She is the sum total of what she has been, and though the specific terms of her identity unfold variously as time passes, the pressure of her history continues to bear upon her present and, to a great extent, determine her future. Nor is spatial remove a solution, whether for Hester or for Huck Finn, whose decision to "light out for the territory" will be qualified by what he has already seen of "sivilization." We Americans, in our literature as in our lives, are a people obsessed with the future, following the grail of the American dream as "we beat on, boats against the current, borne back ceaselessly into the past."[2]

This present-past nexus is an issue that arises with notable frequency in the late plays of Eugene O'Neill, the son of an Irish Catholic immigrant, who inherits a cultural and intellectual legacy which can be traced back to the Puritans. It is almost entirely on these two traditions, the Irish Catholic and the Yankee, that he draws to create the works of his mature period, from roughly 1935 to 1943.[3] During these years, O'Neill was at work on two projects of extremely ambitious scope: one, a cycle of historical plays, the other, a history of a much more personal nature, both dealing with the relationship of past to present. In 1935, having completed *Days without End* and frustrated by a play called "The Career of Bessie Bowen" which would not come right, he began to work in earnest on a series of four plays, set in the latter half of the nineteenth century, about the offspring of characters he named Sara Melody and Simon Harford. Sara was to come from Irish immigrant stock; Simon would derive from a wealthy Yankee family. This merger would produce four sons whose careers in sailing, banking, the railroads, and politics would reflect some of the primary social, economic, and historical developments of the era. It was a project that grew like Topsy; it would not stay within the boundaries of an already ambitious undertaking. As the characters came to life and O'Neill began to trace their line in previous as well as future generations, the cycle expanded to first five, then seven, nine, and eventually eleven plays in all. The final plan was to encompass American history from 1755 to what was then essentially the present, 1932, by tracking the Melody-Harford family history through six generations.

O'Neill worked steadily on these plays up through the final years of the Depression, graphing the characters and their relationships on a huge chart; often he would have several plays going at once. Then in 1939 he put the cycle plays aside and began work on the second project, which was to become a cycle of a different sort. On June 8 of that year he began writing *The Iceman Cometh*, completing it by fall. Within the next four years, he completed *Long Day's Journey into Night*, *Hughie* (part of an intended cycle of one-acts entitled *By Way of Obit*), and *A Moon for the Misbegotten*. These plays draw, often with undisguised directness, upon people and experiences from O'Neill's past—his family, friends from his down-and-out Hell Hole days on the West Side of New York, experiences from his youth and young manhood.

Both sets of plays, the historical and the autobiographical cycles (for the second becomes a cycle in fact, if not in intention), manifest the concern with time noted earlier in American literature at large. Although the ways in which this theme is fleshed out vary from play to play, the interaction of past, present, and future remains a constant concern in both the autobiographical dramas (*Iceman, Hughie, Long Day's Journey*, and *A Moon for the Misbegotten*) and the historical plays (*A Touch of the Poet, More Stately Mansions*, and *The Calms of Capricorn*).

For instance, in *A Touch of the Poet* (the only play of the historical cycle that O'Neill finished to his own satisfaction), the protagonist, Con Melody, is a first-generation Irish immigrant living in New England who has fallen on hard times. He has invested the fortune he brought with him from Ireland in a country inn, which the locals assure him will soon, by reason of its location on a projected thoroughfare, do a bustling business. But the highway never materializes, and Con is left presiding over a ramshackle, out-of-the-way inn, his fortune long gone and his dreams come to nought.

This is a severe tribulation for Con, who was born on an estate in the Old Country and still thinks of himself as an aristocrat. To maintain some shred of dignity, he reinvents himself—not, however, like Gatsby, out of whole cloth. He returns to a climactic moment in his past, when, as an officer in the British army, the Duke of Wellington had singled him out for praise on the battlefield at Talavera. Shortly thereafter he was promoted to major, and life seemed to open before him. He was handsome, fearless, and admired by his peers, and, although he had left a pregnant wife behind on his estate, he was an amorous suitor in the homes of the aristocracy of Spain and Portugal, where as a British officer he was afforded the respect denied him in his native Ireland. "Little did I dream then the disgrace that was to be my reward later on," Con says some nineteen years later.[4]

To salvage his pride, Con insists on living the life of a gentleman. He refuses to work, hires a barkeeper he cannot afford, presses his wife and his daughter Sara into service as cook and waitress, and keeps a thoroughbred mare who is fed even if his family must go hungry. When the effort of maintaining this fiction begins to wear thin, he bolsters his pride with a fascinating act of will and imagination. Standing in front of a large mirror, he recites a verse from Byron's "Childe Harold," which insists that he is among the crowd, but not "of them," that he is superior to the riffraff around him. Con's self-creation also includes a yearly celebration of the pivotal Talavera experience, which takes place during the evening of *Poet*'s action.

Con's dilemma is at base one that stems from the inexorable workings of time. As the clock ticks on, he is removed ever further from that period in his life when dignity was available and dreams seemed within reach. To compensate for the subsequent diminishment he has experienced, he selects an epiphanic moment from his past and tries to bring its fullness to bear on the poverty of the present. But the past, as we will see in chapter 2, does not let Con off so easily.

Simon Harford, who marries Con's daughter Sara, is the protagonist of the sequel to *Poet, More Stately Mansions,* which O'Neill completed through the third draft. (It was revised and published posthumously in 1964 by Donald Gallup and Karl Ragnar Gierow of the Swedish Royal Dramatic Theatre.) Simon, too, tries to conquer time and make himself anew, though he adopts a different strategy from Con's (to whom he is linked by the "touch of the poet" that characterizes both). In the course of *Mansions,* Simon evolves through three different roles, trying on identities, as it were, to see which one fits. As a young man, rebelling against his wealthy father's businesslike approach to life, he retreats to a lake in the woods (an obvious parallel with Thoreau), where he intends to write a book on the natural goodness of mankind and where, incidentally, he meets Sara. After they fall in love and get married, his Rousseauvian idealism lasts a bit longer, but as they have children and their financial needs become pressing, he becomes an entrepreneur and local businessman, much admired by his neighbors (the point at which *Mansions* takes up the story). He still pretends to work on his book in the evenings, but it is clear that he is only going through the motions. As the play progresses, Simon's successes get the better of him, and he hardens into a corporate mogul, even more ruthless and cutthroat than his father. At the same time he is torn between his wife, Sara, and his mother, Deborah, who represent different orientations toward time. When he marries Sara he cuts himself off from his past, choosing to build his future around his wife and sons. But as success possesses him and time carries him forward, he is attracted increasingly by the past and memories of childhood innocence, which he associates with moments spent with his mother in her garden retreat.

In both plays linear time—time of the clock and the calendar—generally brings diminishment and pain. Though superficially Con and Simon have opposite fates, Simon's success is as painful as Con's failure; as even a cursory examination of *Mansions* makes clear, the play traces Simon's increasingly apparent disintegration as he becomes less and less capable of reconciling wife and mother, business and family, self and world. Both characters, beset by present realities they can no longer tolerate, turn to memories of the past as an alternative. And both, as subsequent chapters will point out, ultimately revert to their origins. Con, by play's end, relinquishes his "Major Cornelius Melody" identity and takes on the role of Irish peasant; he "becomes" his father, old Ned Melody. Simon, after duplicating the success of a father he had earlier repudiated, reverts to an even earlier time so that, by the end of *More Stately Mansions,* after a confrontation with Deborah and Sara and a fall in which he injures his head, he returns to his childhood. The innocence he so intensely desires can only be achieved through loss of consciousness.

The theme of past and present is striking in both of these plays, as it is in all seven of the autobiographical-historical plays that culminate O'Neill's career. It brings to mind an oft-quoted line of Mary Tyrone's in *Long Day's Journey into Night*: "The past is the present, isn't it? It's the future, too. We all try to lie out of that but life won't let us."[5]

Because time and its effects are central to the issues dealt with in these plays, we need to consider various kinds of time and the ways in which they function. The most obvious temporal modality is linear or chronological—clock and calendar time. This is evident in O'Neill's plans for the historical cycle as a whole, which was to detail the changes wrought from generation to generation within the Melody-Harford clan, changes within individuals and families as well as broader cultural and historical changes. O'Neill explained that the cycle would portray the characters' psychological evolution in relation to the changing times, showing how developments like the railroads and financial panics affected people's lives. Thus, individual histories meld with the history of the nation. The concept of any history, of course, entails chronicling events as they occur in orderly sequence along a continuum. This linear manifestation of time is of great concern to O'Neill, who meticulously established the time frames of each cycle play according to various historical developments, which he researched with thoroughness and impressive accuracy.[6]

In addition to this attention to chronology in terms of the whole cycle, O'Neill is also extremely deliberate in establishing the time frames of individual plays: from 1832 to 1841 in *More Stately Mansions*, the spring of 1857 to January of 1858 in *Calms*, forty-eight hours in *Iceman*, from morning until midnight in *Long Day's Journey* and *A Touch of the Poet*, from noon to dawn in *A Moon for the Misbegotten*, and between 3:00 and 4:00 A.M. in *Hughie*. In each case this chronological movement is strongly reinforced by the stage directions. We are made aware of the passing of time by changes in scene or physical conditions or both (for example, the ever-encroaching fog in *Long Day's Journey*), as well as the effects that time has upon the characters (Deborah Harford's transformation from a beautiful, youthful woman to a wizened, haggard old "witch," for example, or Mary Tyrone's gradual disintegration and increasingly disheveled appearance).

O'Neill's fascination with chronology is especially evident in *The Calms of Capricorn*, which in 1981 Donald Gallup, former curator of the O'Neill collection at Yale, fashioned into play form from O'Neill's unpublished scenario. In this play, which would have been the seventh of the eleven-play cycle, Simon Harford's son Ethan, the protagonist and captain of a clipper ship, attempts to break the record for sailing around Cape Horn to San Francisco. In so doing, Ethan literally declares war on time. He will prove himself master of the sea or die in the effort. In this play O'Neill emphasizes the interrelatedness of time and space. Historical time is firmly tied to the physical universe; it is, to recall Aristotle's definition, the measure of motion, and its connection with physical movement argues for its relationship to what we commonly call "reality." Thus when Ethan's ship, *Dream of the West*, is becalmed not once but twice in the course of the play—when time stops, as it were—we are not surprised that strange aberrations in behavior and character ensue.

The ticking clock, the emptying hourglass—these are palpable forces in all of O'Neill's last plays and generally the source of great consternation, if not despair, on the part of the characters. Some, like the boarders in Harry Hope's saloon in *The Iceman Cometh,* long for the past, living in memory to cancel the present and to stave off the future. Others, like Con Melody in *Poet* or Erie Smith in *Hughie,* try to re-create the past within the present moment: Con, by conjuring up images of past glory; Erie, by attempting to reestablish a relationship with the former night clerk, Hughie, now dead, via the new clerk, who bears a striking resemblance to his predecessor. In various ways, the characters of these plays locate some ideal in the past. For instance, both Jim Tyrone of *A Moon* and Simon Harford of *Mansions,* as mentioned earlier, long for idealized relationships with their mothers, which have been lost along the way.

This brings us to the second manifestation of time, one that is related to the idea of memory. As time moves relentlessly forward, the characters in these final plays, rejecting what the present offers and the future holds forth, turn with striking regularity to memories of the past. This experience of time is significantly different from that of the linear model and requires further explanation.

When we refer broadly to time, we generally are speaking of linear or historical time, time of the clock and calendar. In this modality, time is perceived as a series of separate and distinct points on a continuum that proceeds inexorably and irreversibly into the future. The present is forever with us, but only as it instantaneously recedes into the past; the future is forever "out there" somewhere. Further, each moment is unique, nonrepeatable, and irrecoverable. The precise configuration of conditions and events it represents will never be duplicated again, if only because another moment has gone by and the universe is one microsecond older. Linear time, then, is a principal feature of the paradigm we draw upon when writing histories; we arrange and describe unique events in terms of their location on a linear continuum.

It is also essential to the paradigm of science. We calibrate units of time with great care and precision: the length of the astronomical year is exactly 365 days, five hours, forty-eight minutes, and 45.51 seconds. Indeed, time and space are two of the principal axes of scientific measurements; the velocity of sound in air at thirty-two degrees Fahrenheit is, for instance, approximately 1,087 feet per second. These examples point to several qualities of linear time. As it is associated with science, it must be predictable, consistent, and absolute (or at least relatively absolute, given Einstein's theory of relativity and the fact that as we approach the speed of light, time slows down). Sensitive formulae calibrated in terms of micro-, nano-, and picoseconds (one trillionth of a second) cannot be approximate; for experimental results to be successfully duplicated, units of time must remain constant.

Thus the determination of standards and procedures for the measurement of time must be agreed upon by the scientific community as a whole, as well as the world at large. Linear time, then, cannot be personal or idiosyncratic. We treat it as external and objective rather than internal and subjective, rational as opposed to arational. It is the modality of time that keeps our society running smoothly.

Yet it is equally true that time is only a construct, that however deliberately scientists may define and measure time in absolute terms, our individual experience of it can and does vary. The daydream, the night dream, reverie, and memory all seem to operate within different time frames. Memory, for instance, allows for reentry into the past. The line thus turns on itself and becomes a circle, as we turn back the calendar and relive episodes and events of our past history. This experience of time remembered, as opposed to our experience of chronological time, is internal, individual, and arational: internal, as it is a function of the imagination; individual, as it is personal and subjective; arational, as it defies conventional rules of logic and predictability.

A construct of time that shares several critical features of memory is that experienced by prehistoric man, a modality that philosopher of anthropology Mircea Eliade terms mythic time. In his study of ancient civilizations, *The Myth of the Eternal Return: Cosmos and History,* Eliade posits that pre-modern (or "archaic" or "traditional") peoples derived their sense of reality by reenacting archetypal actions established by the gods. Only those activities that recapitulated these divine archetypes were experienced as real, as value-laden. These archetypes, cosmogonic in nature and representing a movement from chaos to order, originated outside time, "in the beginning," as it were. Thus, whenever they repeated these paradigmatic activities, archaic men and women experienced themselves as also outside time. Though a great many of their actions were invested with significance in this fashion (courtship, marriage, education, sharing of meals, giving birth), the communal ritual that allowed them to re-create their cosmos was the annual vegetation or fertility rite. Living in close harmony with the seasons, their lives shaped by a yearly ritual to ensure that the cycles of nature continued, their experience of time was cyclic rather than linear. With the aid of ritual, these civilizations returned to the year one over and over again—hence, the *myth of the eternal return.* Eliade thus refers to their overall apprehension of time as cyclic; within the ritual itself they experience what Eliade calls mythic time.[7]

Although this apprehension of time is not identical to that experienced within the context of memory, it does share several of its important qualities. Perhaps the most significant similarity is the notion of returning to origins, of repeating a significant experience.[8] For the archaic society this is done communally; for modern man, it is generally, though not always, individual. In both cases, however, the idea of reliving the past strikes the contemporary thinker as irrational. It defies conventional standards of logic to assume that what is done *can* be undone, or even reexperienced. When Nick says to Gatsby that we can't relive the past, the reader gasps with mild shock when Gatsby replies, "Of course you can." What is past, we are fond of saying, is past.

This is precisely the dilemma of the Tyrones in O'Neill's masterpiece, *Long Day's Journey into Night*. The title itself suggests the importance of time in this play and emphasizes its linear features. As the morning moves inexorably toward night, we watch the Tyrones slowly but steadily disintegrating. As Mary's morphine addiction reasserts itself after an abstinence of two months, the family's fate as a whole seems to be sealed. The others—James, Jamie and Edmund—respond to Mary's relapse in terms reflecting their own loss of hope, and the linear movement is toward a midnight of the soul.

Yet this is only one aspect of time in the play. The linear progression, as well as the spiritual descent that accompanies it, is played off against a retrograde movement that reflects the impact of memory. In the first instance, although time carries the characters forward, they react to one another in terms of past events: the death of baby Eugene, James's drunkenness or miserliness, Mary's former addictive episodes. In addition, Mary, to escape present pain, uses the morphine to move ever further into the past, ultimately regressing to her convent period of girlish innocence. This regression is not the cyclic time of pre-modern societies, communal in nature and established by regularly reenacted rituals which created the world anew. The Tyrones, though their experience is shared, are motivated by individual memories, which splinter the family rather than unify it. The sense of repetition that we experience in their endless arguments, as well as in Mary's regression, which has happened in the past and follows a course that the others know all too well, emerges instead from the view that "the past is the present," that we are doomed to repeat the sins of the past. In this play, time is also measured by repetitive cycles, the constant regression of memory, and a desire to return to the past. Though the particulars vary, a similar movement into the past is evident in *The Iceman Cometh* as well as in the other cycle plays. What, then, are we to make of this series of returns, these attempts to go back to "origins"?

Another variety of cyclic time is explored in a book that O'Neill was fond of quoting and that, as commentators have frequently noted, was extremely influential in his thinking: Friedrich Nietzsche's *Thus Spake Zarathustra*. Nietzsche refers to the doctrine of the Eternal Return in only a few sections of this work, but, brief as they are, these passages contribute notably to the key concepts of the Superman and the Will to Power, since in them the past erects barriers to any attempt to alter the present or shape the future. In book 2, the "Redemption" discourse addresses this problem. Explaining that redemption can only be defined in terms of "redeem[ing] what is past" and by an act of will "transform[ing] every 'It was' into 'Thus would I have it!'" Zarathustra goes on to articulate the dilemma that the Superman faces:

Willing emancipateth: but what is that called which still putteth the emancipator in chains? "It was": thus is the Will's teeth-gnashing and lonesomest tribulation called. Impotent towards what has been done—it is a malicious spectator of all that is past.

Not backward can the Will will; that it cannot break time and time's desire—that is the Will's lonesomest tribulation.[9]

Even Nietzsche's Superman, in exerting his Will to Power, is held in check by time.

The resolution of this impasse resides in the concept of Eternal Recurrence, a teaching which, although it begins with nihilism, ultimately leads to affirmation. We must begin with the declaration that God is dead, Nietzsche insists, since with the existence of God, all things else become "other." This in turn leads to hierarchical judgments, with God defining the center of our existence and relegating all else to the periphery. But the new Dionysian existence wants all things and wants them eternally the same. Thus we must embrace all of our experience, all time and space, all joy and woe, dissolving the traditional distinctions between then and now, here and there, subject and object. All things thus become immanent, and the dualism that results from the acknowledgement of God is abolished.

Nietzsche regarded this concept as his greatest achievement, a triumphant hymn of praise to life, a radical "yes-saying." He makes this exultant affirmation in the following passage from "The Convalescent" in book 3:

"O Zarathustra," said then his animals, "to those who think like us, things all dance themselves: they come and hold out the hand and laugh and flee—and return.

"Everything goeth, everything returneth; eternally rolleth the wheel of existence. Everything dieth, everything blossometh forth again; eternally runneth on the year of existence.

"Every moment beginneth existence, around every 'Here' rolleth the ball 'There.' The middle is everywhere. Crooked is the path of eternity."[10]

Insisting on the unity of all things leads to the abolishment of the past as separate from the present and thus breaks the stranglehold of "it was."

Liberation from the "it was," then, depends on the capacity of the will to embrace all existence in the present. Such an embrace does not renew or re-create, but accepts sweet and sour together. This eternal return is "the willing of *this* life, of *this* moment, of this pain, and in such a manner as to will that it recur eternally, and recur eternally the same."[11]

The reversion to past experiences in the cycle plays does not include this Nietzschean embrace of past and present in an eternal whole. Though the will is there—the characters try time and time again to break the vicious cycles of memory—they fail to rise to the stature of the *Übermensch*. So the cycle becomes rather that of the stoics and the classical historians than that of Zarathustra: an iteration of the same pattern of events with all its limitations and imperfections.

The desire for innocence and a fresh start is finally thwarted. O'Neill's characters, as it turns out, are not Zarathustra's supermen.

The concept of Eternal Recurrence did not, of course, originate with Nietzsche (though his insistence on locating eternity in the present moment is radically new). Nietzsche himself recognized that the idea of the eternal return paralleled the myths of archaic peoples. Their rituals, as we have noted, allowed for the re-creation of the cosmos, not by an individual act of will but by communal action. As they celebrated their annual fertility rites, repeating the ahistorical cosmogony of their divine ancestors, these ancient peoples entered the dimension of mythic time.

Though we have "fallen into history," communal ceremonies that enter this mythic dimension survive in modern religious practice, and, although the particulars vary, religious rituals in contemporary civilization include several important features of the archaic model which bear noting. All rituals assume a preexisting community with shared ideals and require both cognitive assent and volitive consent on the part of its members. That is, the individual participant must apprehend the meaning of the ritual and the values it embodies and freely consent to its power. Stated simply, then, a ritual is an action that embodies and dramatizes the shared beliefs of a community. Because shared religious ideals exist outside of chronological time, the consenting community, as it affirms and enacts these ideals, also exists outside time. Its members experience, at least briefly, Eliade's mythic moment.

It is this function of ritual, I believe, that accounts for the frequency with which O'Neill turns to it in his final plays. As both calendar and memory fail the characters, who see no hope in the future and cannot recover the past, they labor under the tyranny of history; try as they might, they cannot escape. Almost instinctively, as their search for peace reaches its climax, they turn to the ritual of confession, baring their souls to priests of their own making in an attempt to transcend the limitations of time and space.

Whatever the source of O'Neill's vision, whether he draws upon his reading of Nietzsche or dips back unconsciously into the Catholicism of his youth, it seems clear that on some level, as he reaches a critical junction in the action of these late plays, he entertains the possibility of an eternal return, which breaks through the limitations of now and then, of present and past, and he does so by invoking ritual. Act 4 of *Long Day's Journey into Night,* for instance, is structured by the ritual of confession, as all four characters reveal the sources of their present pain. These confessions are not ultimately efficacious in *Long Day's Journey,* or in the play O'Neill wrote immediately prior to it, *The Iceman Cometh;* in other plays we have either parodies of religious experiences (*Hughie*) or quasi-rituals (*A Touch of the Poet*). With the exception of *The Calms of Capricorn,*[12] all of these works, including *More Stately Mansions* (which climaxes with Simon Harford's expulsion from Deborah's Edenic garden), dramatize a return to origins, an "eternal recurrence," suggesting a need for renewal by returning to the source, a version of Eliade's *illud tempus.*

Frequently this return is attempted via memory; an effort to recapture the past by simply willing it, in Nietzschean fashion, through the powers of the imagination. This is essentially the mode of the pipe dreamers of *Iceman,* for instance, who engage in a kind of communal remembering. The stock exchanges and repeated conversations of the down-and-out boarders at Harry Hope's saloon emerge from their pasts, the 1890s (some twenty years previous to the action of the play), when they were gainfully employed or happily married, when life still held forth promise. Unable to accept the fact that this promise has emptied out, they try to cancel out the present by dipping into the past and pretending that tomorrow will bring change.

But their efforts, like those of all who attempt to relive the past, are doomed to failure. In the first instance, memory can be, and generally is, deceiving. The bums of *Iceman* remember selectively. Harry forgets that he hated his wife, Bessie; Jimmy Tomorrow, that his alcoholism drove his wife into the arms of another man; Cecil Lewis, one-time Captain of the British infantry, that he cannot return to his homeland since he was accused of gambling away regiment money. And even if memory were accurate, these epiphanies in the past cannot offer regeneration because they are located somewhere on the linear continuum. Unlike *bona fide* ideals or the myths informing cosmogonic rituals, both of which exist outside of time, memories reside within the framework of clock and calendar. As such, though they seem to offer hope and sometimes do provide temporary solace, the salvation they promise, like the peace that the drummer Hickey peddles, is ultimately fraudulent.

Only within ritual can time be truly suspended and its eroding powers negated, if only for the moment. That moment, however brief, allows the believing participant to nullify the crushing weight of time and begin again, restored and renewed. I use the word "believing" advisedly, since this is an arational experience, one that requires faith. Unlike the rational paradigm of linear time and the voluntaristic mode of memory, mythic time transcends—not denies—reason.

Of the final seven plays, this mythic experience is only successfully achieved in the last to be completed, *A Moon for the Misbegotten.* Written as an elegy for the elder brother whom he both loved and hated, some twenty years dead, O'Neill creates a confessor for Jamie (referred to in *A Moon* as Jim Tyrone) in the person of Josie Hogan, the daughter of an Irish tenant farmer. In the play's climactic scene, Jim, who is tortured by the memory of his drunken debauchery immediately before and after his mother's death and convinced that his return to drink made her glad to die, confesses his sins to Josie in the silver glow of moonlight, and as she becomes, miraculously, at once his mother Mary and the Virgin Mary and Mother Church, the ritual is efficacious and he can lay his guilt to rest at last. He is freed from the tyranny of the past.

This play is suffused with the soft glow of moonlight and the rosy dawn of the following day; its mood is elegaic. The other cycle plays are not so serene, coming to no such closure. All of them, however, explore similar issues: the relationship of past to present, the possibility of either returning to the past or escaping its tyranny, the role of the ideal and the power of the imagination, the hope of transcendence and the desire for peace. It is this last matter that finally unites these plays most essentially, a unity reflected in the circularity of their dramatic structures. With uncanny consistency, this search for peace takes the form of a return to origins: Con Melody's assumption of his father's Irish peasant status in *Poet;* Simon Harford's regression to childhood in *Mansions;* the resumption of former patterns and relationships in *Iceman* and *Hughie,* and Mary Tyrone's regression in *Long Day's Journey.* In these plays the rituals, such as they are, do not finally allow the characters to reclaim the past; they merely return to it and derive whatever comfort it affords, which is, by and large, minimal, since the present insists on intruding and time flows relentlessly on. In *A Moon for the Misbegotten,* however, as Jim returns to his mother in the person of Josie for forgiveness, the sacrament of the confessional brings him peace, for reasons that I shall explain in chapter 7. This peace "surpassing understanding" is the ultimate objective in all of these "eternal returns."

The quest for peace, then, provides the missing link between the two cycles and points to their interrelatedness. As O'Neill searches among the ghosts of his past in these final plays, he, like the prince of Deborah Harford's fairy tale, has been dispossessed. In seeking a way back into the kingdom, the characters and the playwright both are searching for the holy grail, which is available only through mystery and faith.

A *Touch of the Poet:*
Memory and the Creative Imagination

A Touch of the Poet, the only surviving play of the cycle which O'Neill completed, encapsulates the themes that the historical cycle was to treat: the clash
of cultures, the power of the past, the destructiveness of ambition. Set in 1828,
Poet, which would have been the fifth of the eleven-play series, dramatizes the
union of the Irish immigrant Melody clan with the aristocratic Yankee Harfords
through the marriage of Sara Melody, the daughter of Con and Nora, and Simon,
the son of Deborah and Henry Harford. As we reconstruct the stories of Simon's
forebears from O'Neill's notes and work diaries, it becomes clear that each generation in the dynasty repeats in its own fashion the sins of its ancestors; the character
traits and idiosyncrasies of one generation reappear cyclically in the next. At the
same time, we follow the linear progress of succeeding generations, representative of various stages in America's historical evolution. Deborah, Henry, and
Simon Harford, for instance, represent three successive sociological generations
of Yankees (a matter that is dealt with in *More Stately Mansions;* see chapter
3). Deborah is characterized by bizarre aristocratic fantasies that link her with
the decadent European past from which the original Puritans fled; Henry is the
rugged individual, the entrepreneur who builds the family empire; Simon, his
son, rebelling against his father's materialism, places a Thoreauvian faith in nature
and the goodness of the common man.

In Nora, Con, and Sara Melody, the principal characters of *A Touch of the
Poet,* we see three corresponding generations of Irish immigrants. Con was born
and raised on a country estate in Ireland purchased by his father, old Ned Melody,
a "thievin' shebeen keeper who got rich by moneylendin' and squeezin' tenants
and every manner of trick." According to Jamie Cregan, Con's cousin from
Ireland who shows up the day before the play's action takes place, when Ned
had saved enough money, "he married, and bought an estate with a pack of hounds
and set up as one of the gentry" (*Poet* 11). Con's aristocratic past, of which he
is fiercely proud, is somewhat qualified by its origins, as well as by the fact that
he married Nora, the beautiful daughter of peasants on his estate. He achieved

some status by going off to school in Dublin and later rising in the ranks of the British army, where he distinguished himself in battle. But after his promotion to major he was caught making love to the wife of a Spanish nobleman; a duel ensued, and when Con killed the Spaniard, he was forced to resign from the army in disgrace. He took his wife and infant daughter to America to try his fortune but fell on bad times. It is only through the hard work of Sara, now twenty, and the long-suffering Nora that Con is able to maintain his aristocratic pretensions.

In this configuration of characters, Nora, an untutored, hard-working woman who looks old beyond her years, clearly represents the first-generation immigrant. Her Celtic origins are evident in her thick brogue, Irish syntax, and peasant superstitions. Doctors bring bad luck, she says. Although she has abjured her faith to marry Con—she was pregnant at the time and thus married without the church's blessing—she still adheres to the simple belief that her "sin" with Con has brought bad luck upon the family that only a priest can vanquish. Her tolerant attitude towards Con's constant drinking illustrates the typical Irish acceptance of the ubiquitous bottle of whiskey. (Sara's priggishness about drinking represents the other side of this cultural coin.)

Nora's defining characteristic is her selfless devotion to Con, despite his insults and harsh treatment. Her love is the source of her pride and dignity; it is the very core of her existence and gives her life shape and meaning. When her daughter berates her for her slavish obedience to Con's unreasonable demands, she replies, "For the love of God, don't take the pride of my love from me, Sara, for without it what am I at all but an ugly, fat woman gettin' old and sick!" (*Poet* 26). She is an Irish matriarch through and through. As mediator between father and daughter, who are at odds much of the time, she stands at the center of the family unit.

It is this selfless love that wins the admiration of the inn's barkeeper, Mickey Maloy, another first-generation immigrant. Both he and Jamie Cregan prefer Nora to Sara, whom Mickey berates for her "grand lady's airs." What they sense is that Nora remains pure Irish; Sara, who has assimilated American values and mannerisms, has become a stranger in their midst.

Nora, then, along with Maloy and Cregan, represents the first-generation immigrant, still thoroughly Irish and loyal to the motherland. Con's free-loading drinking companions, Roche, O'Dowd, and Riley, also belong to this camp. As such, they retain a certain dignity, even though Con and Sara treat them like peasants. The fact is, they *are* peasants. Yet, though dressed in rags and tatters, they are not as helpless as they might seem. Irishmen all, they use their native wit to maintain a constant source of free whiskey, quite consciously playing peasant to Con's "master." When Con dons his officer's uniform in celebration of the anniversary of Talavera, O'Dowd calls Con "a lunatic, sittin' like a play-actor in his red coat." But when Roche curses him for wearing "the bloody red av England," O'Dowd replies, "Don't be wishin' him harm, for it's thirsty we'd be without him. Drink long life to him, and may he always be as big as fool as he is this night!'' (*Poet* 100). Thus, while Con is using them to play supporting roles in his grand drama, they are also using him.

The second generation is represented by Con himself. Even though he, like Nora, is literally a first-generation immigrant, he acts out the aspirations of the second generation, combining mannerisms and attitudes of the old country with those of the new. For the bulk of the play, Con desperately insists upon his acculturation. He eschews the brogue and calls Sara a ''peasant wench'' when she uses it. He wants America to crush England in the next war (which he feels is ''inevitable'') only to revenge himself on England for disgracing him. Nora, typically, thinks solely in terms of the mother country. When England is driven from the face of the earth, ''we'll free Ireland!'' she says. Melody's contemptuous response is, ''Ireland? What benefit would freedom be to her unless she could be freed from the Irish?'' (*Poet* 40). To identify with America, he must sever ties with his Irish past.

Yet he still retains evidences of his Gaelic blood. It is peasant vitality that informs Con's view that the Yankees are ''fish-blooded'' when it comes to making love. ''They lack savoir-faire,'' he says. ''They have no romantic fire! They know nothing of women'' (*Poet* 62–63). And though he eschews the brogue in Sara and Nora, he himself slips into it unconsciously on occasion. When Riley sings ''Modideroo,'' an old Irish hunting song, for instance, Melody's eyes light up and he ''for[gets] himself, a strong lilt of brogue coming into his voice'' as he recalls fondly the fox hunts on his father's estate (*Poet* 102).

The clearest proof of Con's Irishness, of course, is his response to Henry Harford's insulting bribe when he learns that his son intends to marry Sara. Prior to this point, although Con dismissed Harford as a ''money-grubbing trader'' and a ''Yankee upstart,'' he was sufficiently impressed with the entrepreneur's wealth and power to regard Simon as a suitable son-in-law. But when he discovers through Henry's lawyer, Gadsby, that Harford is opposed to the match and willing to pay him $3000 to move,[1] Con reverts to his Irish ways. Harford becomes a ''swindling trader'' and Gadsby, ''Yankee scum,'' and Con boots him down the street. He vows to duel Harford, even though Sara protests the inappropriateness of this response: ''You're not in Ireland in the old days now. The days of duels are long past and dead, in this part of America anyway. Harford will never fight you'' (*Poet* 125). But his blood is aroused, and his Irish pride must be vindicated. It is this episode that rallies all the Irish townsmen behind Con, though they've taken issue with his uppity ways heretofore; this incident would not be possible if he had totally assimilated American values.

It is significant that Melody's transformation at the play's end is to that of Irish *peasant*. The peasant-aristocrat polarity, like that of the Irish-Yankee one, becomes an axis around which the play's issues cluster. Con's history provides an illustration of the effort to rise through the social ranks, to advance from peasant to aristocrat. Old Ned Melody's efforts to establish himself as one of the gentry are doomed, of course, from the outset, since they occur outside the established social constructs. Ireland had no aristocracy of its own, so Melody tried to simulate the status of the British landowning class which then held sway. When none of the gentry would associate with him, he sent Con off to Dublin with "sloos of money to prove himself the equal of any gentleman's son. But Con found, while there was plenty to drink on him and borrow money, there was few didn't sneer behind his back at his pretensions" (*Poet* 12).

Con finally had to join the English to attain the status he sought. When he became an officer in the British army, he got the chance he wanted "in Portugal and Spain where a British officer was welcome in the gentry's houses. At home, the only women he'd known was whores" (*Poet* 13). Thus, in spite of his father's newly acquired wealth, Con must join forces with the British to achieve social status, and then, only when abroad. Even this does not last; he is ultimately forced to resign his commission in disgrace in spite of his valor in battle.

Because nineteenth-century Ireland did not allow for social mobility, Con left for America. In the land of opportunity and unlimited freedom, a country where "a rich gentleman's son" like Simon could spend a year "living like a tramp or a tinker" (which Nora, with her Irish soul, can never understand), social structures would seem to be nonexistent; a man of Con's wealth and education should rise readily through the ranks. This, however, does not come to pass—a fact which is at the root of Sara's scorn for her father. "He's the easiest fool ever came to America!" she says.

> It's that I hold against him as much as anything, that when he came here the chance was before him to make himself all his lies pretended to be. He had education above most Yanks, and he had money enough to start him, and this is a country where you can rise as high as you like, and no one but the fools who envy you care what you rose from, once you've the money and the power goes with it. (*Poet* 26–27).

Sara, as the third immigrant generation, articulates the American dream with passionate conviction. What she fails to understand is that it is Con's Irish mentality that prevents the dream's fulfillment. "The Yanks swindled him when he came here, getting him to buy this inn by telling him a new coach line was going to stop here," she recalls bitterly. Her anger, which is directed at Con, might be (and on some level, *is*) more appropriately focused upon the "Yanks" who took advantage of the immigrant's ignorance. A stranger in a strange land, Melody did not learn the new ways quickly enough (i.e., he did not become a Yankee) and so lived out the part of the traditional country bumpkin fleeced by the crafty locals.

Stripped of his fortune, Con is reduced once again to the level of peasant (or, more accurately, since an English-dominated Ireland did not allow for any other status, he is forced to acknowledge his true condition). But it is a role he refuses to accept. Desperately fighting to retain a sense of dignity which, for Con, only accrues to the upper class, he insists upon being regarded as a gentleman. He backs Quincy Adams over "that idol of the riffraff, Andrew Jackson" (*Poet* 37). He is not Melody, the innkeeper, but "*Major* Cornelius Melody."

Con has been cast aside—first, by a country that allowed no upward mobility, then by a society which held out a false promise of acceptance. The crux of his cultural dilemma, then, is not just the tension between his Irish and Yankee identities; it is his desire to be an aristocrat in the face of his peasant status. Neither Ireland nor America offers him viable cultural strategies and supports for ascending the social scale; neither system allows him dignity and self-respect. His alternatives are represented in Ned Melody, the "thievin' shebeen keeper," and Henry Harford, the cold-blooded, swindling Yankee trader. Thus it is significant that Con's regression at the play's end is not just to that of Irishman, but to Irish *peasant.* Similarly, Sara's plea that her father be "himself" again is in terms of his aristocratic pretensions: "Talavera—the Duke praising your bravery—an officer in his army—even the ladies in Spain" (*Poet* 178). In the character of Con Melody, O'Neill depicts the cultural dilemma of the Irish immigrant trying to become an American aristocrat. In the process, he dramatizes the complexities of both cultures, examining the dreams as well as the delusions each holds forth.

Sara Melody completes the cultural family portrait, manifesting both Yankee and Irish traits; predictably, she is even more Americanized than her father. Thus it is appropriate that she will bridge the cultural gap in marrying the Yankee, Simon Harford. Her appearance suggests another cultural polarity in the play. The stage directions indicate that Sara has a fine forehead, small ears, a slender neck, and a thin, straight nose, but her mouth is somewhat coarse and her jaw too heavy; she has large feet and broad, ugly hands with stubby fingers. This mixture of peasant and aristocratic features embodies the inner tension of Con Melody, suspended between the worlds of innkeeper and military hero. Indeed, Sara, perhaps the most complex character in the play, includes qualities of all three of the other major characters—Nora, Deborah, and Con.

In many ways, she is Nora's daughter and thus, instinctively Irish. She has inherited her mother's Irish beauty, with her black hair, fair skin, rosy cheeks, and beautiful, deep blue eyes. "Every day you resemble your mother more, as she looked when I first knew her" (*Poet* 45), Melody tells her. Although at first Sara is baffled by Nora's selfless devotion to Con, planning for herself only to "love where it'll gain me freedom and not put me in slavery for life" (*Poet* 25), by the play's end she, too, has surrendered completely to love. Her seduction of Simon, an act which will lead to a hasty marriage, also links Sara with her Irish mother.

At the same time, she is very much her father's daughter and has assimilated his ways. Like Con, she hates the Yankees, who remind her of her lowly immigrant status. For instance, although she can blarney Neilan, the shopkeeper, into holding their bill over for another month, she finds it humiliating to go "beggin' to a Yankee" (*Poet* 28). Yet she regards Riley, O'Dowd, and the others as "ignorant shanty scum" and eschews association with them or the old country. Sara has inherited her father's aristocratic pretensions (hence her desire for him to reassume his Major Melody identity at the play's end); she believes as he does that to advance in America she must sever ties with her Irish past. Her use of the brogue to taunt Con demonstrates this understanding; Melody's aristocratic pretensions, which extend to his dreams for Sara's future, are foiled when she slips into the brogue.[2] Likewise, when he wants to retaliate, he refers to Sara's "thick wrists" and "ugly peasant paws," thrusts which wound her to the quick. Con's aristocratic pretensions, like his ambivalent attitude toward his Irish heritage, are passed down to Sara.

But Sara responds to these pretensions in purely American terms. Significantly, she first appears on stage sitting at a desk checking figures in an account book (in anticipation of the desk she will occupy in Simon's office in *More Stately Mansions*). She is impatient with Nora's superstitious fear of doctors as well as her unwillingness to give her daughter full control of the finances. A pragmatist to the bone, she realizes the impracticality of feeding Con's mare with money reserved for the family; Nora, with her Irish soul, sees only Con's need for the thoroughbred as a symbol of beauty and romance. Clearly, the manager in this family is Sara—shrewd, practical, with her eye on the main chance.

That chance, of course, is Simon, who will enable her to ascend the social and economic ladder. Unlike Con, who is not as concerned with rising above his station as he is in maintaining his aristocratic pretensions, Sara has completely assimilated the success ideology. She will attain more than just the appearance of wealth. And nothing will stand in her way—not even love. When she admits to her mother that she has fallen in love with Simon, she quickly adds,

> But not too much. I'll not let love make my any man's slave. I want to love him just enough so I can marry him without cheating him, or myself.
> *Determinedly.*
> For I'm going to marry him, Mother. It's my chance to rise in the world and nothing will keep me from it. (*Poet* 31)

Thus, too, it is not Con's effort to increase his fortune in New England that Sara reviles, it is the manner in which he fails. Believing that money and education are sufficient to ensure success, she attributes his demise to his own stupidity. "If I was a man with the chance he had," she declares, "there wouldn't be a dream I'd not make come true!" (*Poet* 27). The audience tends to believe her; Sara's determination is matched by a shrewd Yankee pragmatism that has the smell of success about it.[3]

This trio of sociological generations, doubled by the allusions to the Yankee

Harfords (all offstage except Deborah) underlines historical progression and the one-way, irreversible nature of chronological time.

This time dimension is reinforced by the fact that the action of the play encompasses a single day, a pattern O'Neill would later repeat in *Long Day's Journey*. As the devastating effects of that long day are reflected in Mary Tyrone's increasingly disheveled appearance and her regression further and further into her past, so the effects of time's passing in *Poet* can be measured by the changes that take place in Con as morning moves on to night. In *Long Day's Journey* O'Neill uses the structural device of family meals to mark off time and help us gauge the extent of change that occurs as the day unfolds, with the final gathering around the table in act 4 an ironic mockery of the shared after-breakfast laughter of the opening scene. In *A Touch of the Poet*, the markers are the four mirror scenes, which measure not only time but also Con's increasingly desperate and finally futile efforts to maintain his dignity by clinging to his Byronic pose.

In the first mirror episode it is morning, and Con's third drink has just begun to take effect. As he catches his reflection in the mirror, he "squares his shoulders defiantly" and stares into the glass, reciting from Byron's "Childe Harold" as if it were "an incantation by which he summons pride to justify his life to himself." He completes the entire passage:

> "I have not loved the World, nor the World me;
> I have not flattered its rank breath, nor bowed
> To its idolatries a patient knee,
> Nor coined my cheek to smiles,—nor cried aloud
> In worship of an echo: in the crowd
> They could not deem me one of such—I stood
> Among them, but not of them. . . . " (*Poet* 43)

Just as he finishes, Sara walks in. He senses her presence and momentarily loses his composure, but he "immediately assumes an air of gentlemanly urbanity and bows to her," quickly gaining control of the situation (*Poet* 44).

The second incident occurs about half an hour and two drinks later. The stage directions inform us that this is "an exact repetition of his scene before the mirror in Act I" (*Poet* 67). Once again, he completes the chant, but this time he is so absorbed he does not notice when Deborah Harford enters the inn. When she addresses him, "Melody jumps and whirls around. For a moment his face has an absurdly startled, stupid look. He is shamed and humiliated and furious at being caught for the second time in one morning before the mirror" (*Poet* 68). Sara, who has witnessed this scene many times before, is merely contemptuous, a response Melody deflects smoothly. Deborah stares incredulously, then "smiles with an amused and mocking relish" (*Poet* 67), a reaction that is considerably more devastating to Con's self-esteem.

By act 3, it is evening and Melody is drunk. He has endured humiliation at the hand of Deborah and exchanged bitter words with Sara, who embarrassed him in front of his cronies. The anniversary dinner, an annual ritual commemorating the Battle of Talavera, has failed to produce its usual effect, and Con's pride lies crumbled around him. Left alone at last, "his soldierly erectness sags and his face falls. He looks sad and hopeless and bitter and old" (*Poet* 116). But once again the mirror attracts him and he begins the familiar incantation. This time, however, he is only three lines along when a knock interrupts him. The intruder, Nicholas Gadsby, comes with the final blow to Melody's pride—a bribe from Harford to prevent Sara's marriage. This is the turning point for Con. He can no longer maintain his aristocratic pretense when a real aristocrat treats him like a peasant. From this point on, Con responds as an Irishman. True, he insists he will duel Harford, reverting to the tactics of Major Cornelius Melody over Sara's protestation that the days of duels are long past and gone. But his grandiose threat of revenge turns into a fiasco, and Melody and Cregan end up in jail together—an irony that does not escape Con.

Thus the fourth mirror scene becomes a mockery of the three which preceded it. Physically and psychologically defeated, Melody returns from the brawl after midnight, his scarlet uniform filthy and torn, his face and lips swollen and bloody. This time when his eyes fasten on the mirror, he leers into it and says, "By Jaysus, if it ain't the mirror the auld loon was always admirin' his mug in while he spouted Byron to pretend himself was a lord wid a touch av the poet—" (*Poet* 176). He "strikes a pose which is a vulgar burlesque of his old before-the-mirror-one," and, with Nora and Sara as his audience, recites the Byronic passage in a mocking brogue, guffawing contemptuously afterwards. Having put Major Cornelius Melody to rest, he prepares to join his Irish confreres in the bar: "Be God, *I'm* alive and in the crowd and they *can* deem me one av such! I'll be among thim and av thim, too—" (*Poet* 177).

The Function of Memory

The repetition of this mirror scene serves several functions. While it allows O'Neill to shape the action around a central icon, Con's haughty, self-conscious pose in front of the mirror, it also allows the audience to observe the steady disintegration of his Major Melody identity, which depends upon the aloof superiority this ritual is designed to confer. As morning wears on into night and this stance is increasingly difficult to maintain, both Melody and the audience are prepared for Con's ultimate reversion to Irish peasant and his abandonment of his aristocratic aspirations. As such, this progression describes a linear movement. It can be measured, calibrated, divided into units, and its march into the future, like all experiences of historical time, is inexorable and irreversible.

At the same time, memory also plays a crucial role. As Con regards the shambles of his life, his fall from grace—whatever grace he has known—seems complete. Bad business decisions and mismanagement of funds have left him penniless, his dreams come to nought. To salvage what dignity he can, Melody must turn to his days as major of the Seventh Dragoons fighting against the French in Spain and Portugal. As Major Cornelius Melody, Con came into his own, and when that pose threatens to crumble, he performs his ritual incantation.[4] For, as he says to Nora during a poignant exchange in act 2, he has "no future but the past" (*Poet* 63).

The most concrete talisman of that past, of course, is his scarlet full-dress uniform, stored in a trunk in the attic (like Mary Tyrone's wedding gown) and retrieved for the anniversary of the Battle of Talavera, another highly ritualistic sequence at the center of the play which, like the mirror scenes, focuses the relationship between calendar and memory. From all his memories of past glory, Con has singled out one moment which represents value and dignity to him: "the most memorable day of my life," as he tells Deborah Harford. "It was on that glorious field I had the honor to be commended for my bravery by the great Duke of Wellington, himself" (*Poet* 71). This moment becomes an ideal for Con, an epiphany; he regards his life as a gradual but steady decline from that high point—a long slide into the boneyard. Chronological time is thus an enemy, removing Melody ever further from his ideal and the possibility of wholeness.

Thus he turns to memory, which, if his imagination is strong enough, allows him to reenter the past and obliterate the interval between. His Byronic recitations are an effort in that direction, but, as we have seen, the present intrudes in the form of, first, Sara, then Deborah, and finally, Gadsby. Donning his scarlet uniform, however, perhaps because its very palpability performs the requisite magic, allows him to successfully turn back the clock. As he enters the room at the end of act 2 in full regalia,

> he looks extraordinarily handsome and distinguished—a startling, colorful, romantic figure, *possessing now a genuine quality he has not had before,* the quality of the formidably strong, disdainfully fearless cavalry officer he really had been. (*Poet* 88, emphasis mine)

Added to this is the arrival of Jamie Cregan, who was raised on the Melody estate and served as a corporal under Con in the Seventh Dragoons. With Jamie there to serve as chorus, Con reenacts the famous battle in which he so distinguished himself.

His efforts, we realize, are doomed to failure, as the stage action indicates. To re-create the scene, for instance, he rearranges the saltcellar and cutlery on the tablecloth to indicate the enemy lines. Sara, angry after a night of waitressing this drunken party, says in the mocking brogue she reserves for taunting her father,

"I'll have your plate, av ye plaze, Major, before your gallant dragoons charge over it and break it" (*Poet* 97). But even more telling than Sara's interruptions are the intrusions of Patch Riley's Irish songs. Invited to fill out the numbers (though assigned to a separate table), Patch, Paddy, and Dan Roche, having a party of their own on Con's liquor, break into songs which distract Melody from his narrative as, despite himself, his eyes light up and his thoughts return to a still more distant past. As Patch launches into his ballad, Melody "forgets himself," we are told (an interesting phrase), and with a "strong lilt of brogue coming into his voice," exclaims,

> Ah, that brings it back clear as life! Melody Castle in the days that's gone! A wind from the south, and a sky gray with clouds—good weather for the hounds. A true Irish hunter under me that knows and loves me and would raise to a jump over hell if I gave the word! To hell with men, I say!—and women, too!—with their cowardly hearts rotten and stinking with lies and greed and treachery! Give me a horse to love and I'll cry quits to men! And then away, with the hounds in full cry, and after them! (*Poet* 102)

But Sara intrudes once again. The point is that Con's memories, whether of military glory or his life on the old estate, cannot escape both what he has been—his Irish roots (with the peasant retainers an ironic reminder of his origins)—and what he is now, the proprietor of a failing inn. Memory, however powerful, cannot obliterate the past, escape the present, or change the future.

The Failure of Ritual

In casting the mirror scenes and the Talavera celebration in a ritualistic mode, O'Neill, consciously or not, raises the possibility of Con's entering the mythic dimension. But the incantations from "Childe Harold" and the anniversary celebration are more parodies than religious rites—rituals manqué, if you will. Both attempt to reenact the past, to make it present. The mirror scene, repeated four times in the drama, has, as Sara points out, a long history, as does the commemoration of Talavera, which, although it has no litany, has formulaic elements—the specially prepared dinner, for instance, the red coat and the invited guests, along with a narrative of the apotheotic experience.

The uniform suggests a sacramental feature, the outward sign of an inward conversion, and it does indeed produce a palpable transformation in Con, so much so that even Sara, who has witnessed this many times before, is momentarily overcome. The performance, too, has been repeated before; this is the nineteenth celebration of Con's glory, and it is rendered appreciably more meaningful by the presence of Jamie, the symbolic "community" of this event. While the three peasants contribute, however minimally, by simply being there to provide numbers (it is appropriate that they are all male, since the celebration commemorates an all-male experience), Jamie's chief contribution is that as witness and participant in the original event, he can testify to its validity and serve as acolyte. The incantations break down in this regard. Although they have a prop, the mirror, which produces and reflects the hoped-for transformation, the community of believers in this would-be ritual is reduced to one, Con, speaking only to his own image. And in both instances the outside world, the world of non-believers, intrudes.

The quasi-rituals, then, fail in the first instance because they are not truly communal in nature. (It is interesting in this regard that Patch and the others mock Con in the midst of his glory and that he mocks them, mocking him.) The ideal that they celebrate and strive to "make flesh" is individual only—Con's ideal conception of himself—with no communal component, no boon to the society at large, as the archetype dictates. Secondly, and perhaps even more significantly, the ideal moment that Con reenacts exists within, not outside, the boundary of time. It occurred at a given moment in his own history; Con cannot become his own divine ancestor. The powers of memory are only momentary, because Con knows how his story turned out. At the height of his imaginative re-creation, for example, as he says to Jamie, "Brave days, those! By the Eternal, then one lived! Then one forgot!" he cannot forget. He stops at this point, and when he resumes he says bitterly, "Little did I dream then the disgrace that was to be my reward later on" (*Poet* 99). The epithet invoking the Eternal is ironic. There is nothing eternal about Con's glory; even in his memory it cannot last. Thus, neither the incantations nor the anniversary celebration, for all their ritualistic overtones, can work their magic for him. The only possible alternative is the abandonment of his aristocratic dreams and the resumption of his peasant status. He becomes, in the end, Ned Melody's son, not of Melody Castle, but of the shebeen.

Con's Return to Origins

In his return to his roots, it is significant that Con returns to a period prior to his own beginnings. He was born on the estate shortly after old Melody had established himself as one of the gentry. Thus, when he becomes a peasant at the play's end, he claims an identity he associates not with himself, but with his father. The fact is that without his imaginative reconstruction of reality, Con Melody is nothing more than a peasant—and when he arrives at Harford's mansion, he is treated as such. A butler informs Con and Cregan that "Mr. Harford don't allow drunken Micks to come here disturbing him" and that they actually should have come to the servant's entrance (*Poet* 155). Regarded as servants, they respond accordingly, forcing their way into Harford's home and brawling with his three lackeys until the police arrive and evict them. Con himself recognizes the discrepancy between the aristocratic pride that sent him on the mission and the ignominy of the actual event. "Bravely done, Major Melody!" he mutters to himself:

The Commander of the Forces honors your exceptional gallantry! Like the glorious field of Talavera! Like the charge on the French square! Cursing like a drunken, foul-mouthed son of a thieving shebeen keeper who sprang from the filth of a peasant hovel, with pigs on the floor—with that pale Yankee bitch watching from a window, sneering with disgust! (*Poet* 157)

When he is forced to relinquish his pretensions, what he sees is merely "the son of a thieving shebeen keeper." His shooting of the mare, a symbolic suicide, reflects this vision. Speaking of "the Major" in third person, Con explains to Nora and Sara, "He meant to kill her [the mare] first wid one pistol, and then himself wid the other. But faix, he saw the shot that killed her had finished him, too" (*Poet* 169). From this point on, Con speaks and acts the part of an Irish peasant, a transformation which we are meant to understand as permanent.

This cyclic action, the return to Ireland and the shebeen, is not the mythic return of Eliade's archaic man or the Eternal Return of Nietzsche's Superman, but the paradigm of the classical historian who perceives history as a series of repetitive cycles. According to this view, because he is inherently limited, man will repeat the triumphs and the mistakes of those who have preceded him *ad infinitum;* it is an inescapable extension of the human condition.[5]

This view of history helps us understand why we experience Con's final transformation as a loss, which we are clearly intended to do. He lapses into a heavy brogue, and we are told that his face "loses all its remaining distinction and appears vulgar and common, with a loose, leering grin on his swollen lips" (*Poet* 167). He avows he will be "content to stay meself in the proper station I was born to" (*Poet* 179). As he moves into the bar to join the cronies he now accepts as equals, "his movements are shambling and clumsy, his big hairy hands dangling at his sides. In his torn, disheveled, dirt-stained uniform, he looks like a loutish, grinning clown" (*Poet* 175).

One might expect that since his illusions have been maintained at extreme cost—not only to Nora and Sara, but also to Con himself, who as Major Melody must remain aloof and alone, cut off from the warmth of relationships—the abandonment of these illusions would be regarded as a breakthrough, moving Con forward in the fullness of his humanity. In one sense this is true. Con is at last free to respond lovingly to Nora, who, as the play's moral touchstone, has had the audience's sympathy from the start. "Let you be aisy, darlint," he says to her, speaking of the Major in the third person: "He'll nivir again hurt you with his sneers, and his pretindin' he's a gintleman, blatherin' about pride and honor" (*Poet* 168). Shortly thereafter he kisses her tenderly and tells her that he loves her, to Nora's astonished joy; "I've meant to tell you often, only the Major, damn him, had me under his proud thumb" (*Poet* 174).

But Sara (and the audience at large, I would argue) regards Con's relinquishment of his illusions as a diminishment. Desperately, she pleads with him to reconsider. "I won't let you!" she exclaims.

It's my pride too! . . . I know it's my fault—always sneering and insulting you—but I only meant the lies in it. The truth—Talavera—the Duke praising your bravery—an officer in his army—even the ladies in Spain—deep down that's been my pride, too—that I was your daughter. So don't—I'll do anything you ask—I'll even tell Simon—that after his father's insult to you—I'm too proud to marry a Yankee coward's son! (*Poet* 178)

But Con can live in the past no longer. "For the love of God, stop—" he says to Sara. "Let me go!" As he closes the door to the bar behind him, greeted by the welcoming roar of drunken shouts, we are reminded of Deborah Harford's final entry into the summerhouse at the close of *More Stately Mansions*. Although Deborah finally chooses the world of imagination and madness while Con relinquishes imagination altogether, both represent a significant loss. They have exhausted all their other alternatives and close life's door behind them in their final, dramatic exit.[6]

Thus, in both the Con Melody plot and the Sara-Simon subplot, forward movement in time does not bring progress or growth; it merely removes Con further from his ideal moment. To combat the concomitant sense of loss, he travels backward in time to the pivotal Talavera experience, only to discover at last that his military glory cannot be recovered in the world of everyday experience. There is no mythic moment, no satisfactory ritual to transcend this stalemate; Con finally relinquishes his pretensions and accepts the identity of shebeen keeper.

Sara's case might seem to offer some hope. She has begun her climb up the American success ladder. Having seen the ultimate futility of Con's delusions of grandeur, she has set about transforming those dreams into reality in her own life by marrying Simon. She will indeed "wear fine silks and drive in a carriage wid a naygur coachman behind spankin' thoroughbreds, her nose in the air; and live in a Yankee mansion, as big as a castle, on a grand estate av stately woodland and soft green meadows and a lake" as Con predicts (*Poet* 173). But her repetition of Nora's "sin" with Simon (a second cyclic action in the play)[7] calls into question the ultimate outcome of what promises to be a victory. In addition, the fact that Sara acts out of ambition as well as love, plus her comments to Nora about the expendability of the loved one, insisting that love itself is what matters, further casts a shadow over the impending marriage. As Con so accurately predicts at the end of the play, Sara will "have some trouble, rootin' out his [Simon's] dreams" (*Poet* 173), as *More Stately Mansions* will reveal. Con himself will die within a few short years (see note 6).

Thus in this play about poetry and illusion, imagination and its powers, time remains the enemy. The future holds forth dubious promise, and memories of the past cannot redeem the present. It is a dilemma that will haunt O'Neill's characters throughout the historical-autobiographical cycle and will continue into the sequel, *More Stately Mansions*.

3

More Stately Mansions:
Paradise Lost

In act 2 of *More Stately Mansions,* Simon Harford, now thirty-five, the father of four sons and a wealthy and ruthless businessman, returns to his mother's garden, a boyhood haven which he has not visited for many years. Deborah, like Simon, has changed in the interim. Now living with her son and daughter-in-law in the Harford mansion, deeded to them in exchange for Simon's promise to reclaim the family business which his father left in ruins, she has traded her wealth and aristocratic hauteur for the chance to get to know her grandchildren and re-kindle her interest in life.

As Simon glances around the garden, he says with "nostalgic yearning,"

> I had forgotten the quiet and the peace here. Nothing has changed. The past is the present. *Suddenly he turns on her—harshly accusing.*
> You are the one jarring discordant note. The garden of your old self disowns the doting old Granny you have made yourself pretend to be. [1]

This brief vignette touches upon several of the key issues examined in the play. Simon associates Deborah's garden with the past, which represents a peace and serenity he has lost along the way and would like to reclaim. But even in this haven where time seems suspended, change—the snake in the garden—is in evidence. If Simon can't see it in himself, he can at least observe it in Deborah. Whereas before she doted on him, her life now revolves around her grandchildren. Nothing stays the same, and if peace is only available in memories of childhood innocence, Simon is out of luck.

"Don't tell me you are jealous of your children," Deborah replies, with a teasing laugh, enjoying the fact that Simon no longer owns her. This comment points to a second set of issues in the play. As O'Neill presents it here, in order to ensure continued happiness, love requires possession of the loved one. But as soon as this occurs, the loved one, now object rather than subject, is no longer the same, and the relationship changes accordingly.

These two related themes, love as possession and the inevitability of change, impinge directly upon the central action of the play: Simon Harford's quest for peace. If, as Francis Fergusson insists in *The Idea of a Theater,* dramas can be seen as the working out of a single, overarching action or movement, that movement in *More Stately Mansions* is Simon's desperate search for happiness. For Simon, happiness is equated with freedom and self-determination. Yet he finds happiness incomplete without someone to share it. These two thrusts, the desire for freedom and the longing for love, prove to be antithetical here, as in both *A Touch of the Poet* and *The Calms of Capricorn*—and, as far as we can tell, in the other cycle plays as well.

This irreconcilability is related to the question of time past and present, imaged here in the characters of Deborah, Simon's mother, and Sara, his wife, the two women who vie for Simon's allegiance. Deborah, as the opening scene suggests, is associated with the past. For Simon this is linked with his visits to her garden as a young boy, where she would entertain him with fairy tales and they would enact passages from Lord Byron. The garden is linked to the past somewhat differently for Deborah, who spins out elaborate fantasies in which she is the mistress of Louis XIV, and her summer-house, an ivy-covered, octagonal garden retreat, a trysting place which the King had built for their secret rendezvous. In both instances the garden is linked with the past and forgetfulness, with the desire to escape sordid reality and to live a life of the imagination.

The present, in contrast, is associated with "facts," which, although defined differently by the various characters at different points in their lives, are generally tied to physicality and the life of the body, to material wealth. This focus is associated with Sara, Simon's vital, sensual young wife.

The play's action revolves around the struggle of these two women to dominate Simon, to possess his love, tracing Simon through various stages in his life as he identifies primarily with one, then the other of these powerful women. As a young husband and father, still retaining traces of the idealism with which he is associated in *A Touch of the Poet,* his loyalty is toward his wife, and his orientation toward the present and the future. When Deborah returns to his life with the lucrative offer of controlling interest in his father's business and ownership of the Harford mansion, a new balance is established as Deborah and Sara join forces and Simon is excluded, the outrider become out*sider.* He finally attempts to reclaim his dominant position by driving a wedge between them, offering to meet Deborah regularly in her garden once again and inviting Sara to his office, where she becomes part business partner, part mistress (the link is no accident). Once again, the past-present nexus is established: with Deborah he is the little boy returning to the idyllic past via memory; with Sara, he is the driving businessman, thriving on adventure and success and looking to the future. The balance cannot last, however, and as the play reaches its climax—not coincidentally, in Deborah's Edenic garden, where Simon's original fall into time took place—Simon must choose between Deborah and Sara, mother and wife, past and present. More accurately, he must choose between the conflicting desires within himself which O'Neill has concretized in these two women. Deborah represents not just the past, but the life of the mind, of pure imagination and the creation of a new identity by a sheer act of will not unlike that of Con Melody. This represents one road to peace and freedom, but it exacts a steep price: oblivion and madness. Sara offers another route. As she is linked with power and business success, she promises self-sufficiency through ownership, an exertion of the will in another realm.

But always, as suggested earlier, the desire for freedom is hamstrung by the need for love and the impossibility of escaping the workings of time. Although Deborah's garden seems to offer an escape from time in the world of imagination and forgetfulness, and thus one path to freedom from the press of daily life, even here change cannot be avoided. Though nature remains a constant and the garden itself seems timeless, Simon returns to it as a different person, and the mother he finds there is not the one he left behind as a boy. In act 2 he finds her a doting grandmother; still later in the play she will be a wizened old woman, pathetically imitating an eighteenth-century courtesan. Although Simon would like to possess her and, through memory and even madness, if necessary, return to a previous point in his life, chronological time precludes this possibility.

Sara, too, undergoes drastic changes as she sells her soul and her body for Simon's love. In attempting to possess her and thus find fulfillment and peace, along with the wealth and self-determination this option holds forth, Simon once again fails to take into account the changes that come with time. Her transformation is as dramatic as Deborah's. As she becomes his understudy in the business and earns stock in the company by selling him her body, her healthy vitality becomes a coarse sensuality which he ultimately finds repellent. He can no more freeze time than he can possess Sara, or, for that matter, Deborah. Because he cannot integrate the past with the present but feels he must choose, because he sees love and freedom as mutually exclusive, Simon ultimately joins the ranks of O'Neill's self-dispossessed possessors, bereft of both mother and wife and left a little boy, lost in the past.

This conflict between love and independence, past and present, the lure of memory and forward-looking ambition is complicated still further by the historical-cultural underpinnings of the action. As the following pages will argue, Henry, Deborah, Joel, and Simon Harford represent four different stages in America's sociohistorical evolution, parallel to the stages of acculturation represented by the Melodys in the previous play. Moreover, as noted earlier, Simon himself progresses through three stages in his transformation from idealistic entrepreneur to corporate president that strikingly parallel American cultural developments in the nineteenth century. Added to this are the markers and allusions O'Neill carefully weaves into the play to show, according to his stated purpose, the impact of historical developments upon individual lives as these developments intersect with inherited family traits and predispositions. What results is a work that, while it presents us with the history of an individual, Simon Harford, also examines the history of the nation and the philosophical question of the impact of time upon our lives, both individually and collectively.

Autobiographical Elements in *More Stately Mansions*

O'Neill finished the notes, outline, and scenario for *Mansions* in March 1935, immediately after completing the scenario for *A Touch of the Poet*. He did not begin writing an actual draft, however, until April of 1938, having finished drafts of *Poet*, "And Give Me Death," and "Greed of the Meek" in the interim. Although he was making rapid progress on the cycle, this was a period of deep depression for the playwright. It was the O'Neills' first winter in Tao House, their isolated retreat in northern California, and workmen still clattered around the unfinished home. A severe attack of neuritis in early 1938, which left the dramatist unable to work for some time, was aggravated by constant rain for over two months. In spite of these adverse conditions, O'Neill maintained a feverish pace, writing seven days a week. "Working like a man possessed, he would often write straight through the night," Carlotta recalled. "I would find him exhausted in the morning when I brought in his breakfast."[2]

The first draft of *Mansions* was completed, after five months' work, in September 1938. O'Neill immediately began revising and completed a second longhand draft on January 1, 1939; a third, typed draft was finished by January 20. He continued to revise the play throughout 1940 and 1941, during the writing of *Long Day's Journey* and just before beginning *A Moon for the Misbegotten*.[3]

As O'Neill created the Harford family, shut up in his bedroom with its tiny, porthole windows high among the Las Trampas Hills, he also confronted his own past. Excepting *Ah, Wilderness!*, a nostalgic re-creation of his past as he would have liked it, O'Neill had not yet been able to face head-on the ghosts that continued to haunt him. In the subsequent autobiographical plays, he would finally feel free to write more directly about his own family; *More Stately Mansions* maintains a distance through the creation of the Harfords. It is clear, however, that the autobiographical influences in this play, though disguised, are pervasive. For instance, Simon Harford, the protagonist, has qualities that resemble those of the author; he embodies traits both of O'Neill and of his *Long Day's Journey* counterpart, Edmund Tyrone. Likewise, Deborah, Simon's mother, is patterned after Ella O'Neill and has characteristics that will later show up in Mary Tyrone. Sara Melody, Simon's wife, bears striking similarities to Carlotta, O'Neill's wife at that time, and more significantly, is a prototype for Josie Hogan of *A Moon*. There are even parallels between Joel Harford and both Jamie O'Neill and Jamie Tyrone, though this likeness is much disguised.[4]

Critics have pointed out that, because O'Neill is speaking from "behind the mask," in many ways *More Stately Mansions* is even more revealing than his directly autobiographical plays. Sophus Winther, long-time friend and confidant of the playwright, for instance, feels that "*More Stately Mansions* gives a deeper insight into the mind and spirit of O'Neill than any other play he ever wrote."[5] Since the parallels are so marked, it is worth examining briefly the autobiographical details. These connections are most revealing in regard to the playwright's ambivalence toward his mother as suggested by the portraits of Deborah Harford and Mary Tyrone. It is significant, for example, that both Deborah and Mary refuse to accept their sexuality as a normal extension of their roles as wife and mother. While Deborah escapes into daydreams of sexual adventures and Mary into fantasies of virginal purity, both, the playwright implies, are equally destructive. legislating against a healthy maternal response to their sons. Mary's love-hate relationship with Edmund is paralleled by Deborah's response to Simon; her sometimes disdainful treatment of Jamie is mirrored in Deborah's derisive attitude toward Joel.

The clearest indication of O'Neill's unresolved feelings toward his mother as he writes this play, however, is found in the fairy tale of the banished prince which Deborah told Simon as a boy, one which he recalls in vivid detail:

> There was once upon a time a young King of a happy land who, through the evil magic of a beautiful enchantress, had been dispossessed of his realm and banished to wander all over the world, a homeless, unhappy outcast. Now the enchantress, it appeared, had in a last moment of remorse, when he was being sent into exile, revealed to him that there was a way in which he might regain his lost kingdom. He must search the world for a certain magic door. (*MSM* 110)

Just as the king reaches the door and is about to reenter his lost kingdom, the enchantress speaks from the other side:

> Wait. Before you open I must warn you to remember how evil I can be and that it is probable I maliciously lied and gave you false hope. If you dare to open the door you may discover this is no longer your old happy realm but a barren desert, where it is always night, haunted by terrible ghosts and ruled over by a hideous witch, who wishes to destroy your claim to her realm, and the moment you cross the threshold she will tear you to pieces and devour you. (*MSM* 111)

The young king, afraid to open the door and unable to leave it, "remained for the rest of his life standing before the door, and became a beggar, whining for alms from all who passed by" (*MSM* 111). While the fairy tale clearly depicts Simon's desire to regain the childlike innocence he experienced in Deborah's garden, it also suggests the playwright's ambivalence toward his mother—is she beautiful enchantress or hideous witch? O'Neill's diagram of his childhood, included in notes he kept during a brief period of psychoanalysis, provides crucial insights in this regard. The chart reveals that until the age of seven, the outside

world was "practically unrealized" to the young Eugene. At that point he was
sent away to St. Vincent's prep school, banished from the constant presence of
his mother and his beloved nurse, Sarah Sandy. From age seven to fifteen, the
notation reads, "Reality found and fled from in fear—Life of fantasy and religion
in school-Inability to belong to reality."[6] At fifteen, when Eugene learned of
Ella's addiction, the lines of the diagram signifying "mother love" and "nurse
love" come to an abrupt halt and the line designated "reality" begins. These
two pivotal events cast the youth from the warm haven of his mother's protecting
love into the harsh realities of a forbidding world. It was a trauma from which
the playwright would never fully recover.

This complex of emotions, somewhat muted, informs O'Neill's creation of
Edmund Tyrone. Both Deborah's dream world and Mary Tyrone's morphine fog
exclude their sons—a parallel that precipitates the plays' strikingly similar conclusions. When Edmund reaches out for Mary in the final scene of *Long Day's
Journey,* she murmurs gently but impersonally, "You must not try to touch me.
You must not try to hold me" (*LDJ* 174). Deborah, upon entering the realm of
madness in her garden house, responds in the same way. When Simon grabs for
her hand, she flings it away and "with a strange boastful arrogance" says, "Do
not dare to touch me!" (*MSM* 190). Though the tone of Deborah's command
is considerably more strident than Mary's, the impact of their actions is the same.
Both sons, rejected by their mothers, are left beggars, "standing before the door."

While this approach does suggest some fascinating parallels between these
two dramas, however, it ultimately tells us more about the playwright than the
plays.[7] The central issues of *More Stately Mansions,* I would want to argue, are
more cultural and philosophical than biographical in nature. While O'Neill does
seem to be drawing upon real-life models and personal experiences in creating
this fictive world, turning to his own past for raw material, the questions that
the drama raises stem from his intention of tracing a single family through six
generations: How is the individual affected by historical change? To what extent
are we controlled by the past? Are we free to reinvent ourselves with each new
generation, or are we shaped by either the culture at large or our own family
histories? To these matters O'Neill adds his personal conviction that America's
obsession with power and quest for material wealth has been her undoing. These
then become the central issues in the play: the need to possess both wealth and
people, the desire for absolute freedom, and the battle against time.

More Stately Mansions as History

In following the history of the Harfords for roughly two hundred years, O'Neill
intended to tell the story of America's metamorphosis from a group of fledgling
colonies to the most powerful nation in the world. The combination of Irish and
Yankee strains would exemplify the melting-pot process, with the Melody-Harford

family representing a variety of cultural attitudes and values. The growth of the Harford Company from a small milling operation to a conglomerate controlling ships, banks, and consumer outlets and planning to branch out into politics and railroads, for instance, reflects the American conviction that bigger is better and epitomizes our national hunger for expansion. In the *Mansions* portion of this epic, Sara Melody Harford represents the Irish immigrant; Deborah, the decadent Yankee aristocrat; Joel, the bloodless, prim Puritan; and Henry Harford, the prototypical American businessman. Simon, a more complex character, reflects different traditions at each of the three stages of his adult life.

While these phenomena are interesting in and of themselves and reveal O'Neill's acute sensitivity to the influence of cultural forces, they also indicate that the issues of the play are grounded in an awareness of the passing of time and its power. Taken together, the characters present a picture of the cultural-historical evolutionary process. Thus O'Neill presents America's history both directly and indirectly: directly, as he tells the story of America's emergence as a world power through events in the Harfords' lives, and indirectly, as he uses the characters as representatives of cultural types.

We have already seen a sample of this approach in the characterization of the Melodys in *A Touch of the Poet,* literally comprising only two generations but symbolically functioning as three, with Nora the most closely tied to the Old Country, Con responding as a typical second-generation immigrant in his ambivalence toward his Irish heritage, and Sara the most thoroughly Americanized of the three. In *More Stately Mansions* both Sara's Irishness and her Yankee propensities continue to be in evidence. Early in the play her Gaelic qualities seem to receive more emphasis. She is described, as in *Poet,* as Irish in appearance, with a mix of peasant and patrician features. Still very much in love with Simon, she reminds us of Nora in her single-minded devotion to her husband and sons. In contrast to the effete Deborah, she is depicted as vital, healthy, and eager for all life has to offer, characteristics which are linked with her peasant past and her closeness to the soil (an admittedly romantic treatment of the peasant experience). Appropriately, she is six months pregnant when we first encounter her in this play; her fertility and maternal nature, we assume, emerge from her Irish roots. We are also told in the opening stage directions that she has rid her speech of brogue, except in moments of extreme emotion. Thus both physically and temperamentally, Sara is portrayed as a hybrid, an Irish immigrant with American aspirations. She has begun her climb up the ladder by marrying Simon, and she is determined not to lose any ground.

The play's opening scene vividly contrasts Sara's vitality and determination with Deborah's aristocratic aloofness, as O'Neill, in a brilliant bit of stagecraft, sets up the conflict which will structure the entire drama. The action begins in 1832, four years after the close of *A Touch of the Poet.* Simon, now married to Sara and a father himself, has sent for his mother in an attempt to reestablish their relationship, which was broken off with his marriage to Sara. They are to meet at the cabin in the woods where Simon once retired to write his book about the goodness of mankind. Deborah arrives first. Unbeknownst to her, however, Sara has locked herself in the cabin and eavesdrops on the entire conversation. Deborah, the haughty New England aristocrat, is described in some detail. Her appearance suggests the pampered elegance of the privileged class. Though she is forty-five, she looks much younger; her face, we are told, is "astonishingly youthful." Her wavy white hair "gives her the appearance of a girl wearing a becoming wig at a costume ball." She has a dainty, delicate nose, small hands, and tiny feet, and she is dressed entirely in white, with extreme care and good taste (*MSM* 2–3).

As she awaits Simon's arrival, she daydreams aloud to while away the time, providing us our first encounter with her fantasies about Louis XIV:

> The Palace at Versailles—I wear a gown of crimson satin and gold, embroidered in pearls— Louis gives me his arm, while all the Court watches enviously—the men, old lovers that my ambition has used and discarded . . . the women who hate me for my wit and beauty, who envy me my greater knowledge of love and of men's hearts— (*MSM* 4)

We are immediately aware of the contrast between these two women, who occupy opposite ends of the cultural spectrum: Sara, the immigrant aspiring to power; Deborah, the monied aristocrat determined to keep it. The battleground in this struggle will be Simon himself, who arrives shortly thereafter. At this point, the mother-son reconciliation fails, because Simon is still too closely allied with the peasant values associated with Sara at this stage: nature, fecundity, the "good earth." (It is no accident that Sara is in Simon's cabin, a symbol of his Thoreauvian tendencies and his rebellion against his family.) But the battlelines are drawn, here and immediately afterwards, when Sara reveals her presence to Deborah. After Simon leaves, Deborah says to herself, "I have dismissed that Irish biddy's husband from my life forever," a comment not lost on Sara. When she emerges from the cabin, she first speaks in a "polite, carefully considered and articulate English," but it isn't long before she lapses into brogue and says:

> As for what you're after saying about my origin—Don't put on your fine lady's airs and graces with me! I'm too strong for you! Life is too strong for you! But it's not too strong for me! I'll take what I want from it and make it mine!
> *Mockingly.*
> You to talk of honor when in your dream what are you but a greedy, contrivin' whore! (*MSM* 18–19)

Sara's observation is a telling one. It is ironic that while Deborah calls Sara a "vulgar, common slut" (*MSM* 21), in her daydreams she herself aspires to power by becoming the consort of the king. Both women, it should be noted, believe that their access to power must come through a man. Sara, however, acts on this conviction and seduces Simon, while Deborah only fantasizes about it, too removed from life to actually take part in it.

These cultural positions also reflect a kind of historical evolution. Sara, the immigrant, a latecomer to the scene, has to scramble to make her way up the ladder. Deborah's position is more secure. Not only has she been in America longer; her daydreams reflect inclinations and values that associate her symbolically with the Old World from which the original settlers fled. This, of course, cuts two ways. On the one hand, it helps link Deborah and the Harford clan in general to a rank that as closely approximates an aristocracy as anything America will ever know. On the other, the corruption associated with the court of Louis XIV suggests that hers is a power which cannot, indeed, should not, last.

Joel Harford, a minor character who serves primarily as a foil for his brother Simon, can be seen as representing still another cultural type. He is depicted as a straightlaced, prudish Puritan of the H. L. Mencken variety; Con Melody would call him "fish-blooded." Simon himself declares that Joel "isn't a man. He's a stuffed moral attitude," to which Deborah adds that he is "God's most successful effort in taxidermy!" (*MSM* 60). As the colorless, conscience-ridden inheritor of Puritan mores, he has taken on only the grim moral uprightness of his ancestors, with none of their intense fervor. His face, though handsome, is pale—"the face of a methodical mediocrity" (*MSM* 25); his light blue eyes are cold; his voice, dry and prematurely old. Deborah recalls that when she invited him to her garden, "he looked as astounded as if a nun had asked him to her bedroom" and "determinedly recited impeccable platitudes" (*MSM* 11).

Thus, when later in the play Joel registers his disapproval of his brother's immoral business practices, his manner is so stiff and self-righteous that, though Simon may be reprehensible, Joel is the more repugnant. His prissy, puritanical stance is shown in an extremely unattractive light—particularly when we learn that his seeming detachment masks a greedy lust for Sara. Joel, then, typifies the New England aristocrat shorn of his mother's imagination and his father's driving energy. Although he avoids their sins and obsessions, it is only because he lacks the confidence to participate actively in life, choosing instead to watch from the sidelines and pass judgment on those involved in the struggle.[8]

Though he does not actually appear in *More Stately Mansions,* Henry Harford receives enough attention to serve as an illustration of another American type. He embodies the characteristics of the businessman consumed with concern over profits and losses and unable to see beyond that narrow sphere. He is, for instance, fanatically opposed to Andrew Jackson's reelection, which he equates with government "by the ignorant greedy mob." "He wishes Massachusetts would secede from the Union," Deborah says. "One has but to mention the name of Jackson to give him violent dyspepsia" (*MSM* 8). Deborah, also against Jackson's so-called mob, "would . . . be nauseated by their thick ankles, and ugly hands and dirty fingernails, were they ever so noblehearted!"

Henry, on the other hand, is only worried about Jackson's effect on imports and exports. His obsession with business desensitizes him to the needs of others, even members of his own family. Deborah tells Simon that Henry is "much too worried about what President Jackson will do or say next . . . to bother with me" (*MSM* 10). He asks Joel to keep track of Simon's financial successes, a request that even Deborah can see is insensitive. In Henry Harford, then, O'Neill presents us with the fanatic American business executive who labors to extend his financial empire and obsessively pursues total control over his world.

Thus in Deborah, Joel, and Henry Harford we are given representatives of three cultural types. If Deborah is linked with the Old World through her fantasies about the Sun King, Joel is depicted as "Puritanical" (the quotes indicate that this portrait derives from the twentieth century's distorted view of that era), and Henry as a nineteenth-century robber baron, they also provide a rough chronology of American history; i.e., they reflect the play's preoccupation not just with cultural forces but also with the passing of time. I would not want to push this too far, but it is worth noting, for instance, that Deborah's fantasies are about the French, not the English court, which would make the analogue more exact. Nonetheless, the characters do seem to reflect symbolic if not actual generations, as do the Melodys in the previous play.

Simon, a more complex and fully developed character, represents three different cultural configurations as he evolves from idealistic poet to entrepreneur and community leader to grasping, ruthless executive. As a young man in *A Touch of the Poet* and in the early portion of *More Stately Mansions,* Simon resembles the Rousseauvian idealist. After graduating from Harvard, he works for his father's company for a year but soon becomes dissatisfied with the life of a gentleman's son. "He isn't like his kind," Sara explains to Nora in *A Touch of the Poet.*

> He wanted to prove his independence by living alone in the wilds, and build his own cabin, and do all the work, and support himself simply, and feel one with Nature, and think great thoughts about what life means, and write a book about how the world can be changed so people won't be greedy to own money and land and get the best of each other but will be content with little and live in peace and freedom together, and it will be like heaven on earth. (*Poet* 29)

The obvious Thoreauvian parallels,[9] coupled with Simon's frequent allusions to Rousseau, place him in the tradition of the American Transcendentalists, romantics who believe in the essential goodness of man and eschew the class slavery perpetuated by an overly materialistic society. Simon explains to Deborah,

> I still believe with Rousseau, as firmly as ever, that at bottom human nature is good and unselfish. It is what we are pleased to call civilization that has corrupted it. We must return to Nature and simplicity and then we'll find that the People—those whom father sneers at as a greedy Mob—are as genuinely noble and honorable as the false aristocracy of our present society pretends to be! (*MSM* 9)

At this stage of his life he agrees with Jackson and feels that his father's "sneer[ing] at the common people" is "ridiculous snobbery" (*MSM* 8).

His physical description at this point reinforces the sense of nobility he conveys. "He is twenty-six but the poise of his bearing makes him appear much more mature. He is tall and loose-jointed with a wiry strength of limb" (*MSM* 4). He has a "wide sensitive mouth" and "a fine forehead" and his expression, though "sharply observant and shrewd" is also "ruminating and contemplative." That his "long Yankee face" has "Indian resemblances" indicates that he is still sufficiently in tune with nature and the noble savage to balance the Yankee propensity for harsh pragmatism. The two strains in Simon, his practical shrewdness and his poetic soul, are for the moment in equilibrium.

He is, however, unable to maintain this delicate balance for long. While single and independent, he can live alone in the woods, a recluse from society, but when he marries Sara and becomes a family man, he can no longer afford this "luxury." When he meets Deborah in the woods (significantly, his old cabin has fallen into decay from years of disuse), he insists that he has not lost his "poet's dream of a perfect society" (*MSM* 15). But the first signs of his capitulation to the demands of materialism are already evident. He has neglected lately to work on his book (as Deborah points out, "four years is a long 'lately' ' "); he now plans to write as soon as he and Sara have enough to retire. When Deborah poses the critical question, asking whether they have decided how much is enough, he hesitates, then lies and says, "Yes, of course" (*MSM* 16). He is even beginning to look like his father—an ominous portent.

When we see Simon four years later, he is in the second phase of his evolution. "There is a noticeable change in the impression his personality projects," the stage directions indicate, "a quality of nervous tension, the mental strain of a man who has been working too hard and puts unrelieved pressure on himself" (*MSM* 43). He has just decided to give up his book, believing now that "Rousseau was simply hiding from himself in a superior, idealistic dream" (*MSM* 46–47). The discrepancy between his poetic aspirations and his business preoccupations has become too great to bear: "There I was at night in my study trying to convince myself of the possibility of a greedless Utopia, while all day in my office I was really getting the greatest satisfaction and sense of self-fulfillment and pride out of beating my competitors in the race for power and wealth and possessions!" (*MSM* 46). He now calls Jackson a "mad fool" whose "insane banking policy is ruining the country" (*MSM* 47), he is thinking of increasing his retirement goal of one hundred thousand dollars, and he dreams of expanding into shipping and banking by taking advantage of failing firms. The insidious process has begun; Simon has acquired an unquenchable thirst for power. The poet-idealist whom for a time "the town considered . . . the most talented of its young merchants" (*MSM* 15) can no longer maintain an indifferent attitude toward his business success. As Deborah predicted in the woods, the means is rapidly becoming the end.

By 1840 Simon has been completely transformed into a grasping executive who feeds off the failure of others. His expression is "habitually tense," his manner, "curtly dictatorial"; he speaks "rapidly and incisively" (*MSM* 69). Whereas once he could take pleasure in the simple pleasures of fatherhood, he now sees his sons as servants of the Company: "Ethan as manager of our marine division, Wolfe to direct the banking branch which we will own before long, Jonathan as our railroad executive, and Honey our representative in politics" (*MSM* 84). He is brutal with his brother and Tenard alike; "the only moral law here," he says, "is the strong are rewarded, the weak are punished" (*MSM* 71). The Rousseauvian ideal of pure freedom has been transformed; Simon now believes that "the possession of power is the only freedom" (*MSM* 74). The reversal is complete as he tells Sara and Deborah, "What is evil is the stupid theory that man is naturally what we call virtuous and good—instead of being what he is, a hog. . . . In a nutshell, all one needs to remember is that good is evil, and evil, good" (*MSM* 172).

Simon's three stages are not, of course, separate and distinct. One blurs into the next, implying an inevitability about his transformation from idealist to materialist, from dreamer to destroyer. The Thoreauvian paradigm clearly fails. It is not a viable alternative to success in business, but merely a youthful phase of naive wishful thinking. The ultimate inefficacy of this alternative is underlined by its parallel with Deborah's fantasies. Simon himself makes the connection when he says to Sara, "Rousseau was simply hiding from himself in a superior, idealistic dream—as Mother has always done, in a different way. . . . It was really her influence that made me first conceive the idea of my book, I can see that now—her haughty disdain for Father because he was naturally absorbed in his business. And yet all the time she owed everything to his business" (*MSM* 47). Linking Simon's idealistic dreams with Deborah's daydreams of freedom through power points to the inevitable subversion of his idealism. He is converted from his mother's dreamy detachment to his father's greed; both extremes, the play suggests, are destructive.

Time as the Enemy

While time's passing is implicit in the sociocultural stages represented by the characters as types, their characterization as individuals stresses this theme even more directly. All three major characters undergo radical transformations in appearance as well as values in the course of the play, as a reading of the stage directions at the beginning of each act quickly reveals. Simon's transformation has just been examined in some detail; those of Deborah and Sara are equally striking.

It is apparent from the opening scene that Deborah regards time as her enemy. She is obsessed with aging and the inevitable loss of beauty that it brings. This is particularly crucial to Deborah, of course, given her belief that her only access to power resides in her ability to manipulate men. Thus, although we are told she looks much younger than her forty-five years, as she waits for Simon in the opening scene, she says bitterly to herself, forcing a self-mocking smile, "What can you expect, Deborah? At your age, a woman must become resigned to wait upon every man's pleasure, even her son's" (*MSM* 3). She sees herself not as a mother looking forward to meeting a son she has not seen for four years, but a woman being kept waiting by a man. She consoles herself by saying, "Age? You harp on age as though I were a withered old hag! I still have years before me." But the critical question, as Deborah herself realizes, is what she will do with those years. Until now she has spent her time dreaming away behind the safety of her garden walls, but now, as she tells Simon, she is afraid that life has passed her by. When he protests, Deborah responds,

> While you are still beautiful and Life still woos you, it is such a fine gesture of disdainful pride to jilt it. But when the change comes and an indifferent Life jilts *you*—Oh, I realize I am hardly as bad as that yet. But I will be, for I constantly sense in the seconds and minutes and hours flowing through me, the malignant hatred of life against those who have disdained it! But the body is least important. It is the soul, staring into the mirror of itself, seeing the skull of Death leer over its shoulder in the glass! (*MSM* 12)

Time, the ultimate antagonist, brings only death. Deborah says it all when Simon first asks her what has happened to make her seem so sad. "Nothing has happened," she responds, "except time and change."

Time will bring more changes before the play is over to both Deborah and Sara, who, like Simon, move through three distinct, if overlapping, stages in the course of the play. These stages do not, like Simon's, represent a kind of historical evolution, though they do reflect shifts in cultural values. As they are accompanied by alterations in appearance, however, they insist upon the "ever whirling wheels of change."

As we have noted, Sara is originally described as a beautiful young mother, still closely allied to her ethnic heritage though anxious to leave her poverty behind; as such she regards Deborah as the enemy. During the second phase of the action, however, the cultural polarities these characters represent—peasant vs. aristocrat, Irish vs. New Englander—will be neutralized as each takes on qualities of the other.

When Deborah offers Simon the Harford company and Sara, the Harford mansion at the end of act 1 in exchange for a chance to become acquainted with her grandchildren, she turns from her fantasy world of the past and embraces life in the present. At the prospect of this new purpose in life she exclaims: "I can love again! Oh, I may surprise myself, I think, with my undreamed-of talents as a good woman! Already at the mere prospect of escape, I feel a rebirth stirring in me!" (*MSM* 40). The fertility represented by Sara's cultural heritage is transferred to Deborah as she adopts her daughter-in-law's Irish values. That Deborah begins to feel a "rebirth stirring" in her reflects the fecundity that derives from Sara's native vitality—a sharp contrast to the decadence embodied in the New England aristocracy. Thus as act 2 opens, Deborah, now a contented grandmother, is described in terms that resemble her daughter-in-law. Her body and face have filled out a little and her expression is described as one of repose and inner harmony. Significantly, her eyes and smile still retain their old ironic aloofness and detachment; the transformation has the potential to reverse itself (as indeed it will).

Sara, on the other hand, absorbs some of Deborah's qualities. When we see her after four years as mistress of the Harford mansion, "her manner has taken on a lot of Deborah's well-bred, self-assured poise, and her way of speaking copies Deborah, although the rhythm of Irish speech still underlies it." She is also dressed much better, expensively and with discriminating taste. Her smile "has lost its old passionate tenderness and become entirely maternal" (*MSM* 75). Deborah and Sara have, in short, become one. Although this does provide domestic unity of sorts, it excludes Simon except as an amusedly tolerated son and provider. Because he is necessary to support their lifestyle, Deborah and Sara grant Simon nominal status as a family member, but he is essentially excluded from their intimacy. It is his duty to confront the outside world and wrest from it sufficient wealth to protect his women and children from the harsh realities of life. In the process, as is so frequently the case, Simon becomes an outsider. Sara and Deborah, once immigrant and aristocrat, are now united as mother and grandmother; they share the joys and responsibilities of childbearing and present a unified front which excludes Simon.

Realizing this, he decides to drive a wedge between them in order to divide and conquer, ushering in the third phase of the action. Since their polarities have been neutralized by Sara's new brood of Harfords, Simon attempts to reverse this process. He first transforms Sara, the Irish peasant-become-aristocrat, into a Yankee by making a contractual agreement with her, as mentioned previously. Inviting her to his office, he agrees to incorporate her into the business by giving her stock in the company in exchange for sexual favors, transforming her, in essence, from wife to prostitute. Simon's rhetoric reinforces the crass commercialism of his offer. He tells her that she will have to be shameless, to strip herself naked and accept her own greed so that she can go on without "false scruple" and take what she wants from life. "I know you will find the game I play here in the Company as fascinating a gamble as I find it!" he adds. "A fascinating game—resembling love, I think a woman will find" (*MSM* 91). Business and love are equated, and both are reduced to the level of a game.

As might be expected, Sara's evolution into a Yankee during the next year is paralleled by a striking change in her appearance. By the third act her face has a bloated, dissipated look, with dark shadows under her eyes. Her mouth seems larger, its full lips redder, its stubborn character become repellently sensual, ruthlessly cruel and greedy. Her eyes have hardened, grown cunning and unscrupulous. Her manner varies between an almost masculine curt abruptness and brutal frankness, plainly an imitation and distortion of Simon's professional manner, and calculating feminine seductiveness. (*MSM* 139)

As her identity merged with Deborah's in an earlier stage, she now takes on Simon's characteristics. Her harsh responses to Joel, for instance, are an extension of Simon's derisive manner. In the scene with Tenard, whose bank has just been absorbed by their company, Sara sits in Simon's chair and proceeds to humiliate the banker as ruthlessly as her husband would have. She has "become" Simon, as Sara herself finally recognizes with horror.

At the same time, Simon resumes his visits to Deborah's garden, reestablishing the mother-son relationship that existed before his marriage. Deborah's decadent fantasies reassert themselves, and she once again sees Sara as a "filthy slut." Her appearance, like Sara's, has changed drastically, although only a year has elapsed since the previous act. The stage directions here are worth quoting at some length. As she once again waits for her son,

her small, girlish figure has grown so terribly emaciated that she gives the impression of being bodiless, a little, skinny, witch-like, old woman, an evil godmother conjured to life from the pages of a fairy tale. Her small, delicate, oval face is haggard with innumerable wrinkles, and so pale it seems bloodless and corpse-like, a mask of death, the great dark eyes staring from black holes. She is dressed in white, as ever, but with pathetically obvious touches of calculating, coquettish feminine adornment. Her beautiful white hair is piled up on her head in curls so that it resembles an eighteenth-century mode. Her withered lips are rouged and there is a beauty-spot on each rouged cheek. There is an aspect about her of an old portrait of a bygone age come back to haunt the scene of long-past assignation. (*MSM* 161)

O'Neill, never one to flinch at asking the impossible from his actors, creates in the part of Deborah an incredibly demanding role. Within a few short hours of stage time, she must change from a youthful forty-five to a "witch-like old woman." The audience, witnessing this transfiguration, is made inescapably aware of the ravages of time. Deborah has become the "withered old hag" she mentioned with such fear in act 1. Sara likewise undergoes radical changes with the passing of time.

The Allure of the Past and the Search for Salvation

It is important to recall that within these configurations, Deborah is predominantly associated with the past, while Sara is linked with the present and future. In the play's opening act, for instance, Simon's loyalty to Sara and his sons represents a commitment to the new life he is building and a movement away from his paternal family. As Yankee executive later in the play, Sara is also symbolically associated with the present and the future, linked to the company which continues to expand, spreading outward in ever-widening circles. This growth, depicted as an inevitable outcome of success, is essentially a linear phenomenon, one-way and inexorable. That, in fact, is precisely Simon's problem: success leaves him feeling empty and hungry for another triumph; greed begets only greater greed.

Deborah, on the other hand, except for her grandmother phase, is consistently linked with the past. When Simon can no longer ignore the fact that his ever-growing material wealth has left him spiritually impoverished, he turns increasingly to Deborah for salvation. This represents a movement away from the present to the past, from linear time to memory. To combat a present he cannot tolerate and a future that holds forth no hope, he seeks to escape into forgetfulness and oblivion. Like the lost prince of the fairy tale, he seeks reentrance into the kingdom.

I use religious language here deliberately, since in the final analysis, Simon's quest is a spiritual one.[10] The lost kingdom of Deborah's fairy tale has all the earmarks of the kingdom of heaven, and Simon's amassing of wealth has actually been an effort to obtain salvation (though he is only dimly aware of this, at best). Like his Puritan forefathers, Simon has sought certitude of his election, which takes the form of his continually expanding empire. When he embraces the financial goals and business ethics of his father, Simon is operating under the aegis of secularized Calvinism, which would argue that financial success is a sign of salvation.[11] The difficulty lies in the fact that he can never be sure the amount of wealth amassed is sufficient; to borrow Deborah's words, Simon never knows ''how much is enough.'' The covenant of grace has been replaced by a spurious and secular covenant of works, and the certitude of salvation lies always just beyond his grasp. The greater his success, the more spiritually bereft he becomes, as he tells Joel in act 2, ''I concentrate all my mind and energy to get a thing done. I live with it, think of nothing else, eat with it, take it to bed with me, sleep with it, dream of it—and then suddenly one day it is accomplished—finished, dead!—and I become empty . . . as if I had lost my meaning to myself'' (*MSM* 72).

When he discovers that he cannot obtain salvation through the amassing of wealth, he turns inward, back to the family, to his wife and mother for assurance of grace.[12] Because he has dichotomized his own tendencies as pragmatist and poet in splitting Sara and Deborah, however, integration and peace of mind are even farther out of reach. Neither woman can save Simon; he has corrupted them both. Ironically, although they once again represent cultural extremes, Sara, now the business executive and Deborah, the decadent aristocrat, both bear the same marks of moral decay. The womanliness of mother and wife alike has been subverted into an instrument for possessing Simon, and their passion, duplicating his thirst for power, becomes rapacious greed. Because they are obsessed with owning Simon, neither is capable of saving him.

It is clear, however, that even when Deborah was the detached dreamer of an earlier stage in her life, unconcerned with power beyond the realm of her fantasy kingdom, she was incapable of offering Simon salvation. Her daydream of pure freedom, with its Calvinistic underpinnings linking it to the past,[13] is ultimately inefficacious in the present: the play demonstrates that neither her romantic visions nor Simon's Transcendental idealism provides a viable strategy for coping with life experience.

Thus all the alternatives that the play has dramatized are exhausted as *Mansions* moves to its climax. Simon's moral and mental schizophrenia has driven him to such a desperate state that he suggests to each adversary that she murder the other. The steadily widening gap between the positions represented by Sara and Deborah can no longer be bridged, and Simon feels wrenched asunder. Unable to integrate the extremes of his nature and aspirations, he must destroy one or the other. Culturally, he must choose between Deborah's aristocratic fantasy world and Sara's ambitious Yankeeism; psychologically, between the female principle represented by Deborah's poetic romanticism and the male principle of Sara's powerful aggressiveness; emotionally, between mother and wife, past and present.

Thus, when Simon finally confronts Sara and Deborah, temporarily reconciled, he blurts out violently that "if the conflicting selves within a man are too evenly matched," he must choose one or the other. At last he finally sobs exhaustedly, "Can't you see you are driving me insane?" and the two women comfort him as one:

> *Deborah:*   Our beloved son!
> *Sara:*   Our husband! Our lover! (*MSM* 175)

Gratefully, Simon turns to Sara and says, "I love you, my mother"; to Deborah, "I love you, my—." The dash here is significant. O'Neill has demonstrated on several levels the ultimate impossibility of the Sara-Deborah merger, whether as peasant and aristocrat, mother and grandmother, or Yankee and New Englander. If Simon is to enter the state of grace, i.e., if he is to achieve the peace that comes from wholeness and inner harmony, he has only one alternative—reverting to a preconscious stage where there is no knowledge of sin or guilt.

At this point then, Simon, rejecting all those dimensions of experience that he associates with the ticking clock (that is, which we as audience link with historical time)—Sara, the present, his ambition and goals for the future—turns to memory as his last hope. Images of childhood beckon Simon like a mirage hovering on the horizon, as he recalls a period of his life which now seems a golden age. Thus he turns to Deborah, who holds the key to the past; it was she, after all, who expelled him from the kingdom of innocence with her tale of the banished prince. But he must do more than turn back the clock; he must return to a period which precedes his fall into consciousness and history. This can only be accomplished by entering Deborah's summer-house, which throughout the play has been associated with madness. In act 1 Deborah herself, on the brink of insanity, casts out her "devil," the old Deborah, and in a symbolic gesture, shoves her into the summer-house and shuts the door, saying, " 'Depart from me, ye cursed!' " In this instance it would seem that the summer-house represents not just forgetfulness but a kind of hell. But to Simon her Temple of Love (which one generation earlier Evan Harford called a Temple of Liberty) holds forth freedom, since it will free them both from Sara, as he tells Deborah: "We will leave her here. We will go together so far away from the [sic] reality that not even the memory of her can follow to haunt my mind. You have only to open that door—" (*MSM* 181).

Because entering the summer-house represents an abdication of consciousness, it promises freedom from guilt. Deborah's garden becomes for him the Garden of Eden where he once walked in prelapsarian bliss. When forced out of Paradise and into the world of adulthood with its attendant ills, Simon lost a peace that he could not replace. He says to Deborah, in religiously laden language,

> I have waited ever since I was a little boy. All my life since then I have stood outside that door in my mind, begging you to let me re-enter that lost life of peace and trustful faith and happiness! You once drove me out, and all that has happened since began. Now you must either choose to repudiate that old choice and give me back the faith you stole from me, or I will choose her! (*MSM* 182)

His mother becomes the angel barring the gate to heaven.

Simon's desire to escape the harsh realities of his present existence operates on several levels. Biographically, it reflects the playwright's longing to assuage the sense of homelessness that has haunted him since his exile to St. Vincent's as a boy of seven—the same emotion that informs the return-to-the-womb motif found so frequently in O'Neill's canon. As O'Neill writes this play he, too, turns to the past for answers. In terms of the dramatic action, it is Simon's desire to resolve his inner conflict by escaping into memory. From a spiritual perspective, it represents an effort to eradicate guilt by returning to Eden. This in turn reflects the "radical innocence" of the American that Ihab Hassan writes of; the continual quest for the virgin land, the "green breast of the new world" that "year by year recedes before us." It is also linked with Deborah's decadent fantasies of a love retreat, a spin-off of the romance tradition—the mythos of summer, as Northrop Frye terms it (hence Deborah's "summer-house"). "The perennially childlike quality of romance," according to Frye, "is marked by its extraordinarily persistent nostalgia, its search for some kind of imaginative golden age in time or space."[14] For Deborah the golden age is located in the resplendent era of Versailles; for Simon, in the warm haven of youth. For both the impulse to recapture this past focuses on the summer-house.

It is appropriate, then, that the climactic scene of this play is set in a garden. Linear time and all its ramifications have failed Simon. Contrary to popular

American mythology, things do not seem to be getting better with time. The world of "facts" and "reality" with which this mode of time is associated in *Mansions* is a grim one. When, after the opening scene, Deborah believes she has lost Simon forever and tries to "face facts," for instance, it takes the form of her forcing herself to acknowledge her declining beauty and encroaching old age, of determinedly asking her husband whether President Jackson's feud with the U.S. Bank has had an adverse effect on business. The result of all this "factuality" is that Deborah shrivels up, literally and figuratively. Likewise, when in act 3 Sara becomes as pragmatic and goal- (i.e., *future*-) oriented as Simon, she becomes ruthless, not herself. Linear time brings diminishment and disillusionment.

Memory, or a similar reconstruction of life (for that is essentially what memory offers), appears to be a more viable alternative to Simon as the play reaches its climax; hence, he returns to the garden which holds such symbolic significance for him. This deliberate return to a scene associated with an earlier time in his life recalls Con Melody's equally determined effort to salvage meaning in his life by returning to the past. With Con, this is associated with two key rituals (or rituals manqué)—the re-creation of the Battle of Talavera and the recitation of Byron's poem. (Byron is also linked to Deborah's garden, reinforcing the connection between memory and imagination, the need to withdraw from everyday affairs and transcend the limitations of chronological time.)[15]

Simon and Deborah, however, have no ritual to help them in their efforts to enter another world, though Deborah's fantasies seem to have approached that function.[16] The closest Simon comes is his memory of the banished prince fairy tale, which is more an icon than a ritual. But as icon, it serves a key function: he has determined that to achieve peace at last, to regain the kingdom, he must enter the summer-house. He will do this, we note, with Deborah at his side, though the fairy tale would have it that the enchantress waited on the opposite side of the door. The implications of this detail are ominous, since we recall that Deborah herself believes that her mad counterpart resides inside the summer-house, waiting to devour her—or, we assume, anyone else who enters.

The garden has other unfortunate connotations. As it is associated with nature we would expect it, like the woods of the opening scene, to be timeless, to partake of eternity. But unlike Simon's woods, Deborah's garden is not, in fact, "natural." O'Neill describes with extreme care (and detailed sketches) the artificial atmosphere that prevails here. The garden is separated from the outside world by an eight-foot brick wall. The summer-house is entirely covered by ivy—it is hidden, disguised; a row of Italian cypresses, out of place in this New England setting, lines the wall. The door to the summer-house is painted a Chinese lacquer red, another incongruous detail.[17] The shrubs are all clipped into geometrical shapes—cones, cubes, spheres, pyramids, and so forth, and in front of the house is a small reflecting pool. While this garden suits Deborah's fantasy world with its formality and Versailles touches, it is not an apt setting for a return to nature, simplicity, and innocence, if this is Simon's intention.[18] The world of imagination as we see it limned here is an unreal one.

This in itself casts doubt on the efficacy of Simon's effort to escape the present by a return to the past, a turn from "facts" and the present moment to a world of pure mind—or even madness.

The hope held forth by the past does indeed prove to be fraudulent, as the final action reveals. Just as Simon and Deborah are about to enter the summer-house and retreat into madness, Sara appears. Simon, childlike, does not recognize her. "How dare you trespass here?" he demands. "Do you think my mother's garden is a brothel?" Because he experiences the garden as a state of union with his mother, the intrusion of Sara as wife-mistress contaminates its purity, turning it into a brothel (which, we recall, was its symbolic function in Deborah's fantasies). Realizing what is about to happen, Sara offers to leave Simon if it will save him. "You can have him back!" she tells Deborah. "I'll go away! I'll never trouble you again!" (*MSM* 188). Echoing Christ's "Greater love hath no man than this, that a man lay down his life for his friends," Sara says, "You know no woman could love a man more than when she gives him up to save him!" (*MSM* 188). It is a gesture that the aristocratic Deborah cannot understand.

> Deborah [*Stares at her, unable to believe her ears*]: You really mean—you will give up—go away—?
>
> Sara: I will—for love of him—to save him. I'll sign everything over to you. All I'll keep is the old farm, so I'll have a home for my children, and can make a living with them. I'll take them there tomorrow. (*MSM* 188)

At this evidence of Sara's strength, Deborah is vanquished. She retreats into the summer-house alone, becoming again the disdainful consort of the king and flinging away Simon's grasping hand: "Do not dare to touch me!" she says. "Get back to the greasy arms of your wife!" (*MSM* 190). As Deborah shoves Simon down the steps and knocks him unconscious, Sara whispers in horrified awe, "God help me, she's done it! Ah, it's a great noble lady you couldn't help proving yourself in the end, and it's you that beat me, for your pride paid a price for love my pride would never dare to pay!" (*MSM* 190).[19]

Simon, however, remains lost in the past. Because there is no absolute standard for success (read "salvation") in Simon's scheme of things, because he cannot know "how much is enough" and cannot tolerate not knowing, he must at length regress to a state of total dependency. Thus, when he regains consciousness after his fall, it is as a little boy. In an ironic reversal of his symbolic fall into consciousness when Deborah banished him from her garden, his fall into unconsciousness as Deborah pushes him down the steps results in his return to a preconscious, childlike state. He says to Sara in a child's voice, "I fell and hit my head, Mother. It hurts" (*MSM* 194). Sara, then, has become "mother" to Simon; it is the only level on which he can accept her love. And in Irish fashion, she is willing to accept this maternal role. "Yes, I'll be your Mother, too, now," she says with a "fierce, passionate, possessive tenderness," and "your peace and your happiness and all you'll ever need in life!" (*MSM* 194). She will be the *axis mundi* of Simon's world.

Thus Simon's return to his origins, to a past which seems to hold forth harmony and wholeness, offers only the false peace of oblivion. What is missing in this play is some means of transcending both the structures of linear time, with its unforgiving inexorability, and the limitations of memory, which requires an abdication of the present and a refusal to acknowledge change. Religious and communal rituals, when efficacious, can provide such an alternative, as in the case of the prehistoric tribes Eliade describes whose ritualistic returns to the beginning of things allowed them to re-create their world.

The garden symbology thus suggests one final alternative, most conspicuous perhaps by its absence. Simon, dealing with a vague, nameless guilt that threatens to engulf him, is everyman; as the banished prince, he is Adam seeking readmittance to the garden. According to Christian doctrine, Adam's sin is finally cancelled with Christ's sacrifice; the promise of the Garden of Eden is fulfilled in the garden of the empty tomb. But nowhere in this play—unlike the others that were to follow (with the exception of *The Calms of Capricorn* and *Hughie*, where the final scene is cast in religious terms, but ironically)—is the ritual of confession or another overtly religious ritual made available, in spite of the fact that Simon's dilemma is clearly, at base, a spiritual one. Simon remains vanquished by time and mortality. In seeking to buy his way into the kingdom and relying on the possession of both wealth and people to secure happiness, he ultimately loses everything he has sought: power, financial security, independence, freedom. He has even lost his mother, though he has gained a substitute in Sara. But in doing so, he must become a child. His return to origins is not salvific, but merely regressive. And this, as the first act of *The Calms of Capricorn* reveals, proves as unsatisfactory as we would expect. Simon's final days are spent living with Sara on her farm, relying on her industry and resourcefulness. Occasionally he pretends to retire to his cabin by the sea to write, but his book (entitled "The Meaning of Life") consists only of blank pages. He finally gives up the pretense and joins his son Honey, a tin peddler, on his route. Like Con Melody, with whom he is linked, his spirit has been broken and he dies a relatively young man, a possessor, self-dispossessed.

4

The Calms of Capricorn:
Race against Time

The Calms of Capricorn, originally the starting point for the historical cycle, eventually became the fifth play in a projected nine-play cycle (later, the seventh in
the final, eleven-play projection). According to O'Neill's master plan, *Calms*
would be the first of four plays devoted to Sara and Simon Harford's four sons:
Ethan, Wolfe, Jonathan, and Honey. Ethan, the sailor, would be the protagonist
of *The Calms of Capricorn,* O'Neill's clipper-ship play; Wolfe, the gambler-
turned-banker, would be the principal character in the second, "The Earth Is
the Limit"; Honey's rise and fall as a politician would provide the focus for the
third, "Nothing Is Lost but Honor"; and Jonathan's railroad career would be
outlined in the fourth, "The Man on Iron Horseback." According to Bogard,
"The Earth Is the Limit" was set in San Francisco and the Sierra Nevadas between 1858 and 1860; Sara was to appear and would have been fifty-three at the
end of the play. Honey's story would be dramatized in San Francisco, New York,
and Washington during the Civil War and Reconstruction years, 1862–1870; Sara
would be sixty-two by this play's end. Jonathan's play, "The Man on Iron
Horseback," which covered a period from 1876 to 1893, was set in New York,
Paris, Shanghai, and the midwestern United States. It was to include Sara's death
at age eighty-five.[1]

O'Neill worked steadily on the cycle from 1935 to 1939, moving back and
forth in time on the ever-expanding project as his health and energy permitted.
As late as May of 1941, he notes in his *Work Diary* his plan to expand the cycle's
first two plays, "Greed of the Meek" and "And Give Me Death," into four;
he subsequently outlined these four plays and rewrote *A Touch of the Poet* and
More Stately Mansions in light of his new scheme. Finally, however, early in
1949, he was forced to acknowledge defeat because of the tremor in his hand
and generally poor health; he would never complete another play. At his home
in Marblehead in 1951 (1953, according to some sources), he destroyed most
of the notes and drafts of the cycle plays—an incalculable loss to the history of
modern drama. Some of the manuscript material escaped destruction, however,

and was added to the Yale Collection that same year. Among this material was a complete scenario for *The Calms of Capricorn.*

Donald Gallup, for thirty-three years curator of the Collection of American Literature at Yale University, has turned this scenario into a finished play, incorporating, wherever possible, the dialogue it included. His objective in reconstructing *Calms,* as he explains in his introduction, is to make it more readable and hence increase its general accessibility. This he has done with great faithfulness to the original scenario, which he also transcribes and appends to the play. The finished product, in making this work available to O'Neill scholars and all other students of American drama, is a significant contribution to our understanding both of the cycle specifically and O'Neill's work methods in general.

Certain qualifications must be made, however, before setting out to discuss this work. First, it is by no means a finished play. We have ample evidence from the various versions of earlier completed plays, O'Neill's *Work Diary* and notebooks, as well as his own comments, that he revised extensively from one draft to the next. It was his habit to include everything in the early drafts—lengthy descriptions of the characters, their thoughts and motives, explicit and often overwritten dialogue—then prune, trim, and shape through various versions until the final product contained in condensed and focused form all that the earlier drafts spelled out.[2]

Such is the case with *More Stately Mansions,* which is extant in drafts and, like *The Calms of Capricorn,* does not represent O'Neill's final effort. In the earlier play, however, we are at least working with O'Neill's own draft (shortened by Karl Ragnar Gierow and edited by Donald Gallup). With *Calms,* we are working only with O'Neill's scenarios. Though Gallup uses the dramatist's own words whenever possible, he acknowledges that his version is undeniably a far cry from a finished product. On occasion, for example, the playwright had several different ideas about a scene; where it should take place, who should be present, what should be said, whose speech should conclude the scene or act. Thus any attempts at close textual analyses or specific comments about the shape of the action are ill-advised, at best.

What we can examine on solid ground are the themes the work sets forth. Since these themes are all taken directly from the scenarios, not from Gallup's adaptation, and, further, appear in various forms throughout the other cycle plays (as revealed in the *Work Diary,* notebooks, and two extant dramas), it seems safe to assume that we are dealing with primary material. We are extremely fortunate in having even this limited option available to us, since the *Calms* scenario offers us our only direct (or almost direct) experience of the third Melody-Harford generation (the fifth *Harford* generation if one goes back to Jonathan, Simon's great-grandfather). In draft form, it provides invaluable information and insights about the cycle enterprise as a whole.

The play, which occurs primarily aboard the *Dream of the West,* a clipper ship bound for San Francisco and the California gold mines, begins in the spring of 1857 on Sara Harford's farm, where she and Simon have been living for sixteen years. The opening act provides a link between this and the previous play, *More Stately Mansions;* Simon dies of pneumonia, and the four Harford sons, now in their twenties, decide to take Sara west on Ethan's ship to begin life anew.

The plot concerns Ethan's driving ambition to become captain of a clipper ship and set a new record for the voyage from New York to San Francisco via Cape Horn. As the title suggests, however, nature is no mean antagonist; the calms, with their ironic connotation of serenity, will prove to be his undoing. O'Neill uses the calms and Ethan's battle with the sea both to shape the action and to focus the issues of the play.

At the journey's outset, fate seems to be on Ethan's side, as the first mate, Hull, who suffers from a heart condition, has not appeared for duty and Ethan is promoted to fill his position. Hull arrives at the last minute, however, and Ethan, forced to resume his second-mate status, is stung by rage and jealousy. Goaded by the mysterious and provocative passenger Leda Graber, he responds to Hull's insults with a smashing blow; Hull falls, hits his head, and dies, and the wheels of fate are set in motion.

Ethan's ambition to beat the record is at first held in check by the ship's captain, an older gentleman named Payne who has sailed with Hull for forty-five years. His allegiance, like that of the dead first mate, is to the ship and its passengers, not to the sea. (The significance of Hull's surname is fairly obvious here.) At first all goes well; the winds favor them and Payne makes record time to the Line. As the ship's owner, Warren, a passenger on this voyage, points out, it is almost as if "the Captain was forced into a record, he even seemed to resent it" (*Calms* 50). But as they languish day after day in the calms that settle in just north of the Tropic of Capricorn, the passengers, previously content with the ship's progress, become increasingly critical of Captain Payne and grumble about his unwillingness to take risks. A subplot also builds, as Payne's young wife Nancy, in love with Ethan, longs to be free of her elderly husband. Payne takes a severe fall and is critically injured; the guilt-ridden Nancy nurses him back to health. Ethan, now in charge, becomes the focus of the passengers' increasing animosity as the calms continue, until on the twentieth day, driven to their limits by a sense of helplessness and frustration, Ethan and Nancy finally murder her husband as he sleeps. Just then, a squall is sighted and the winds come up. For the duration of the voyage, Ethan, now captain, makes record time until the ship is just outside San Francisco harbor, when the second calm descends and robs him of his victory. On this level, then, the calms serve as Ethan's antagonist, delaying the voyage and so controlling his destiny. It is not so much the sea he must defeat as the calms.

The calms also seem to shape the attitudes and values of those on board. As the primary action unfolds, we learn a great deal about the passengers, principally Nancy Payne; Wolfe, Jonathan, Honey, and Sara Harford; the ship's owner, Theodore Warren, and his beautiful daughter Elizabeth; Ben Graber, an embezzler, and his seductive companion, Leda; and the Reverend Samuel Dickey, a Protestant minister. Initially their behavior is governed by fairly conventional standards. The women, especially Nancy and Elizabeth, reject the sensual and outspoken Leda as socially and morally beneath them; at this point appearances still carry weight. Nancy pretends concern for her husband and Elizabeth acts disinterested in Jonathan, while the unctuous Reverend Dickey spearheads a general disapproval of the on-going card game as well as Leda's promiscuity. During the first calm, however, their behavior begins to change. The psychologically disorienting effect of apparent timelessness, of endless days with no change or prospect of change starts to take its toll.[3] The pressure builds steadily, and social conventions begin to crack under the strain. Warren, whose cheating at cards is obvious to everyone, flies into a rage when Graber wins all his money, while Wolfe, no longer able to maintain his pose of indifference, moves to the table to watch Warren accept Ben's winnings as a "loan" and begin the game anew. Reverend Dickey casts aside his pious facade and sleeps with Leda, confessing both his adultery and his religious doubts to the young Elizabeth (after she rebuffs his advances). She, in turn, admits her fascination with Leda and, on Leda's advice, sets out to seduce Jonathan. Nancy and Ethan, also succumbing to Leda's influence, acknowledge their passion and eventually murder Payne.

Leda's amorality, in short, is in the ascendency. When a squall appears on the horizon, promising wind, the passengers, as if by general consent, seize upon it as a sign of divine approval of Ethan's leadership and give themselves over to Leda's ethical system, one which eschews pretense and advocates openly seeking what one desires.

However, what in Leda is essentially amoral, a philosophy tempered by an unexpected selflessness and ennobled by her passionate commitment to honesty, in the others becomes selfish, grasping, and opportunistic. Early in act 4, as the ship nears its destination, the stage directions state flatly that everyone has become totally *im*moral. While the passengers all assume that Nancy and Ethan hastened the captain's death, for instance, their reactions range from mild amusement ("We'll let the happy lovers keep their little secret," says Warren) to outright approval (Jonathan: "It's a fine victory for Ethan. . . . The end justifies the means"). Warren is only mildly concerned that Ethan has wrecked the ship with his wide-open sailing, since he plans to "tinker her up to run okay" and sell her on the strength of her record, and everyone approves of his good "business sense." "I'm proud of my father," Elizabeth says; "he'd cheat the devil" (*Calms* 99). She, in turn, openly acknowledges her illicit relationship with Jonathan and her gratitude to Leda. Sara unabashedly dreams of wealth and power, as, in his fashion, does Reverend Dickey.

All this is destined to change. When the second calm descends as they near the Golden Gate, a series of reversals is set into motion. As it appears increasingly likely that they will not break the previous record, set by the *Flying Cloud,* one by one the passengers begin to question what has transpired. Warren, always quick to complain, thinks aloud, "I wonder if this calm isn't the punishment for Ethan's crime and Nancy's and Leda's lust" (*Calms* 105). Dickey, reembracing his pious platitudes, concludes that God is punishing them; Elizabeth viciously calls Nancy a murderer, and Sara, suddenly getting religion herself, agrees.

It is as if all their decisions hinged on the challenge Ethan hurled at the sea. If he could defeat the forces of nature, on his own terms and in however unscrupulous a fashion, then they were justified in pursuing their own destinies in equally ruthless fashion. When Honey, always the politician, very reasonably points out that Ethan's loss has no effect on them, that they will land by morning and there is still plenty of gold left in the hills (and whiskey on the clipper), Dickey's suggestion of throwing Nancy and Ethan overboard to purify the ship seems suddenly ridiculous. The point is that they have implicitly assumed that their fate was bound up with Ethan's. Hence, the whims of the sea have controlled not just his fate, but theirs, as well. O'Neill, then, uses the calms to shape the action of the play as well as the attitudes of the characters, whose ethical systems change with the changing winds. When nature seems to withdraw her approval, their bold declarations of moral independence crumble like a house of cards.

The audience, viewing this phenomenon from a safe and critically detached distance, sees it quite differently. O'Neill is not suggesting that a god resides in nature, doling out rewards and punishments according to some determinable code of behavior. We realize that the winds' appearance at the moment of Payne's murder is no more nature's approval of Ethan's act than the final calms constitute a punishment. Nature, in the last analysis, is indecipherable, aloof and indifferent to man's petty schemes and machinations. Any meaning we impose on her is a construct of our own devising.

At the same time the drama suggests the need for some code of behavior or system of beliefs with which to evaluate our experience and upon which to base moral choices. And if an amorality based on nature proves inadequate for the characters, so does the conventional system with which they begin and end the voyage. Their return to a religious stance at the play's end is not meant to win our approval, since its fruits are dissent, hatred, hypocrisy, and very nearly murder, as they rush to throw Ethan and Nancy overboard in order to purify the ship. O'Neill presents us with a Hobbesian universe: without a moral code or a set of shared principles, chaos will inevitably ensue. But the conflict in the play suggests that the old standards have fallen away. The traditional god no longer will serve, and neither science nor gold nor love can take his place. This, we may recall, was the starting point for the *Dynamo* trilogy (1929), which eventually expanded into the eleven-play cycle: the search for God in a godless universe. In *The Calms of Capricorn,* we see that search in all its complexity and despair.

As the above plot summary makes clear, time, while it is an obvious concern in *The Calms of Capricorn,* functions differently here than in the other cycle plays. While it operates on the thematic level in the other historical and autobiographical dramas, lying at the heart of the characters' anguish, in *Calms* it is more explicit. Essentially an agent of the action, it is more obviously the antagonist for Ethan than, for example, Con Melody or Simon Harford. In the other plays that he was composing during this period (O'Neill first recorded the idea for *Calms* in his notebook in 1931 and worked on it intermittently at least through 1939), time is one of the threads of life's tapestry; here it is warp and woof. The whole phenomenon of the calms, for instance, treats time as an almost physical entity. Like the oxygen we breathe, it is most noticed in its absence. Once again, this calls to mind Aristotle's definition of time as the measure of motion.

For the passengers and crew of the *Dream of the West,* all movement seems to have ceased. The ship appears to be suspended in space—there are no stars or sun with which to calculate their latitude and longitude, no breeze or movement of any kind; they are blanketed by a stifling, almost palpable heat. It proves an unnerving experience. Tempers and temperaments are tested to the breaking point. With time suspended, something must give, and it does.

Perhaps because of *Calms'* unique treatment of chronological time, memory and ritual play a reduced role. This will be discussed in some detail later on. It is sufficient to say at this point that, although allusions to past events and relationships are made (chiefly by Sara) and repetitive events and character traits do occur, the characters of this play are not compelled by a desire to return to the past or even a need to escape the present. Thus the overarching cyclic movement of the other six plays does not structure this drama. Likewise, *Calms* does not employ a religious ritual to purify and renew society. Because it presents time so differently, *Calms* merits our full and careful attention.

Ethan's Race against Time

The clearest instance of linear time and the one that structures the plot is Ethan's race for the record. For Ethan, freedom and peace are linked to conquest of the sea. When Sara asks him early in the play what he wants, he replies that he wants nothing, but what he needs and would gladly pay the world for is "victory over the sea—and so, freedom and rebirth." He goes on to say, "Someday as captain of a ship I shall fight her storms and calms and fogs and crosscurrents and capricious airs and make a faster voyage around the Horn to the Golden Gate than ever man has made—as a last gesture of victory, now when the era of American triumph over the sea is dying from this money panic of the greedy earthbound'' (*Calms* 15). To be the master of his fate, he must defeat the sea. The universe itself becomes his battleground, then, and the terms are defined in space and time: the distance from New York to San Francisco must be covered in fewer than eighty-nine days, twenty-one hours. Fate for Ethan is inextricably bound to this challenge.

Nancy is equally concerned with time. She is acutely aware of her relative youth compared to her husband's age. The play repeatedly emphasizes that he and Hull, with whom he is linked thematically, are of another generation. Various passengers comment on this, generally by attempting to dissociate themselves from the aging captain. The forty-eight year old Warren, for instance, insists that he is much younger than the captain and that Payne is too old to be a husband, much less the skipper of a ship. On the other hand, Leda, when flirting with Payne, hits the essential note by saying, ''You're not old to me'' (*Calms* 42). The image is of the hourglass emptying itself. Early in the play, as he stares at the dead Hull, Warren admits that ''one sees there is so little time left, and one has missed so much'' (*Calms* 42).

This is precisely Nancy's fear, that life will pass her by. In love with the young and vital Ethan, she focuses her resentment on her husband. ''He'll never die,'' she cries. ''He'll want me to go to bed with him, the fool, the disgusting old fool'' (*Calms* 63). Thus while Payne lives, time, in equally urgent fashion, is Nancy's enemy. Even though, both before and after Payne's fall, it is clear that his death will not be long in coming, Nancy and Ethan cannot wait. They decide to cheat time and murder Captain Payne while he sleeps. Both quests— Ethan's for victory over the sea and Nancy's for love—come together in this action. Ethan now becomes captain, securing his chance to break the record, and Nancy is free to marry him. The question then becomes whether there will be time to enjoy their freedom.

Progress, with its thrust toward the future, also impinges on Ethan's quest. As Ethan himself realizes, the era of sail is rapidly giving way to that of steam. Seen through the eyes of someone like his brother Jonathan, Ethan's romantic attachment to sailing is an anachronism. Unlike Ethan, who has inherited ''the touch of the poet'' from his father Simon and his grandfather Con, Jonathan is the Yankee pragmatist, shrewd, cold-hearted, with his eye on the main chance. O'Neill shapes the issues around these contrasting positions. Evolution will have its way; the wheels of history will grind on. But what will happen to the individuals in history's path; what values and aspirations will be sacrificed to historical necessity?

Both Ethan and Jonathan seek mastery over their own fate. As in the other cycle plays, freedom is the prize above all others. For Ethan, the terms of freedom involve mastering nature through an exertion of his will, whatever the price. Jonathan would agree with the need to be free as well as the necessity for conquering nature; it is Ethan's method he would question. Why rely on the caprices of wind and wave, when the steam engine will soon tame the sea. Or better yet, look to the railroads (which, of course, O'Neill already had in mind for Jonathan's play, "The Man on Iron Horseback"). If Ethan retains links with his grandfather's Irish poeticism or Simon's transcendental tendencies, Jonathan has inherited the pragmatic Yankee strain, looking to technology and progress for answers. Ethan is linked to the past; Jonathan, to the future.

A third alternative is represented by Honey, the youngest of the four sons, who combines elements of both positions. Another pragmatist, he will take the road most likely to lead to success (he spends the voyage insinuating himself with the gold-seekers, intending to strike it rich in the mines), but, unlike Jonathan, he is not without feeling. Ethan says at one point, "I like you, Honey," and it is Honey who evidences most concern at Ethan's impending suicide at the play's end. To the extent that he is a kindred spirit of Ethan's, Honey is linked with his Irish background; indeed, the stage directions tell us he is "all peasant Irish," and he leaves the stage after his first appearance singing "The Praties They Grow Small," calling to mind another Gael, Phil Hogan of *A Moon for the Misbegotten*. As he is also like Jonathan, however, Honey adopts a forward-looking, progressive approach. Even his name cuts both ways: "Honey" is an Irish nickname, yet in terms of imagery, it is linked with the gold that he hopes will make him rich. The most adaptive one of the lot, he has all the makings of an excellent politician (which, again, is what O'Neill has in mind).

Reinforcing these contrasting positions are the songs of two opposing groups in the supporting cast, the sailors and the gold-seekers, as O'Neill provides a counterpoint of background sound effects to reinforce the stage action. Though we do not actually see either group, their presence is frequently acknowledged, and their songs bring an affective weight to bear on the issues at hand. Early in act 4, for instance, Ethan seems to have defeated the sea. He has made record time from the moment he assumed control of the ship. As they near the end of their journey, the gold-seekers' song dominates "a subdued, beaten sea chanty" (*Calms* 99). When a second calm descends just outside San Francisco, however, one that will ultimately foil Ethan's effort to establish a new record, the sailors' sea chanties are again ascendant. The subliminal effect of hearing one song over the other in the background, (a technique O'Neill experimented with in *Emperor Jones*) asserts the tension between the old romanticism and a novel, hard-headed progress.

A related historical motif is suggested by the name of the clipper ship, *Dream of the West*.[4] The West offers a new beginning, the chance to start life over again. In this regard mention is made of the "panic" (presumably the panic of 1857),[5] which is associated with the Eastern financial establishment, a closed fraternity available only to the wealthy. The gold rush presented an alternative for those who felt disenfranchised by the power structure of the East. Nuggets were lying in riverbeds just waiting to be sifted from the sand; Honey promises to give Leda a hatful. The dream of the West promised an entirely new way of life, with a whole new set of possibilities—another future-oriented option.

Thus the emphasis on the future in *Calms,* which beckons to the characters in various ways, sets it apart from the other plays of this period, which tend to be dominated by the past. Simon Harford's expanding empire in *More Stately Mansions* does look to the future, as we have said, but that proves unsatisfactory and he ultimately returns to the peace of childhood. The forward-looking posture of *Calms* seems appropriate, given the shift in values and the exchange of tradition for technology. Nonetheless, the possibility that freedom and happiness lie ''out there somewhere,'' not in the past, is, among O'Neill's plays of this period, unique to *Calms.*

This play is most like the rest of the cycle in its treatment of freedom through possession, a crucial issue. Ethan speaks of the sea as a woman—aloof, indifferent, unscrupulous, and compelling. If he can conquer her, he says, he will cast her aside with scorn; if he loses, he will gladly sacrifice his life at her altar. The terms are his own, and the quest is for freedom, which to Ethan means becoming sole master of his fate.

The play offers several other routes to independence. Sara, still the Irish matriarch turned Yankee (her return to roots at the end of *More Stately Mansions* seems not to have held), argues that freedom comes through wealth and power. To this end she plans to relocate in the West, where she hopes that her family will prosper; in this same spirit she sees Elizabeth Warren, the wealthy shipowner's daughter, as a promising match for her Jonathan. Love is not a serious consideration in her reckoning; marriage is primarily a business arrangement. Jonathan couldn't agree more. If a wife can provide the financial backing that will send him on his way, he will guarantee her a good return on her investment—as long as there are no emotional strings attached.

Wolfe, the second son, is closer in temperament and inclination to his older brother. Like Ethan, he is of a reflective, philosophical, even wistful bent. He has no trouble understanding Ethan's passionate commitment to his dreams and is probably the first to intuit his decision to commit suicide. ''I understand,'' he tells his brother quietly as Ethan says farewell. But though their goal is the same, he has chosen an opposite path in its pursuit. The only freedom is to feel no need, he insists. He has deadened himself to all emotions—love, passion, greed, desire. Life is a game that he refuses to play; he even expresses disinterest in his constant game of solitaire. (When he joins the ongoing card game at the play's end, Wolfe's aloofness has broken down; O'Neill is setting up the next play, in which Wolfe will enter into the struggle for power.)

Several women in this play, as in the other cycle plays, seek freedom through conquest of another sort: love. In possessing their men, they will have access to power and hence, freedom. This has its roots in Sara's relationship with Simon, made explicit variously in *Poet* and *Mansions*. We even see her saying at his funeral, "He had a lovely soul . . . if he'd have only given me that soul how I would have loved and protected it!" (*Calms* 24). Elizabeth follows directly in Sara's footsteps, as does Leda, in her own way.

The only exception appears to be Nancy, whose love for Ethan does not seem to emanate from a desire for power. Although she does want to own his love (and hence, him), she is willing to assume all the blame for their crimes and thereby set him free if his happiness requires it. She willingly goes to her death with Ethan—even gladly, seeing his suicide as final proof that he loves her. Thus her freedom comes through love; sounding much like Nora Melody she tells Ethan, "Hell with you will be heaven, if you only love me" (*Calms* 120).

The range of philosophies represented here is not as significant as the fact that all the characters, whatever their vision of life, seek freedom through possession. Whether the possession is material (Sara, Jonathan) or spiritual (Ethan), whether it is focused in relationships (Elizabeth, Leda, and, in a different way, Nancy) or the refusal of relationships (Wolfe), to possess one's soul one must possess something outside it, too. "But what shall it profit a man," we hear O'Neill asking, "if he gain the whole world and lose his own soul?"

The difficulties these characters encounter in their search for happiness lie precisely in the irreconcilability of their double goals: freedom and love. For to live beyond limitations demands imperviousness to the needs of others; once they love and are loved in return, they become automatically vulnerable and no longer self-contained. Ethan and Wolfe try to deny their need for others, but the play tells us this decision cannot hold against their longing for love. Jonathan will be more successful at it, being less fully human, but the cost for him will be even greater than for his brothers. "You'll be a great success in the world, Jonathan," Ethan tells him, "but a horrible failure in life" (*Calms* 115), and it seems safe to assume that "The Man on Iron Horseback" would have borne that out. Thus the American nemesis, as O'Neill sees it, is in identifying freedom with possession.

Memory, Cyclic Time, and Ritual

Cyclic time in *The Calms of Capricorn* is manifested chiefly in the recurrence of family traits and characteristics. Both Ethan and Wolfe inherit their poetic, contemplative nature from their father Simon; paradoxically, Jonathan also inherits his capacity for a businesslike approach to life from his father. It is as if the two facets of Simon's nature have been divided among his sons.[6] Sara has also contributed her share to Jonathan's materialistic nature; the predilections of both parents merge in their offspring. Other instances of this recurrence include the sons' wives, now linked thematically with Sara. A clear example is Elizabeth's speech to Nancy as she contemplates her marriage to Jonathan. She says, "You and I will be like sisters and Sara will be our mother and we will help our men take possession of the world—and we will possess the world by possessing them'' (*Calms* 101). It could just as easily be Sara explaining her intentions to Nora.

These individual character traits, recurring in each new generation, cluster around the cycle's most predominant theme, possession and self-dispossession. Each new generation seeks possession in its own manner, redefining terms and means, and each is ultimately dispossessed.

Unfortunately, we can only imagine how this theme would have been played out in the remaining cycle plays. In *The Calms of Capricorn* we watch Ethan struggle toward his goal, only to have victory snatched from him at the last moment, although his final dispossession involves a moral victory in the end. Though he realizes that he doesn't love Nancy, he cannot bear to hurt her. He decides to commit suicide, plunging into the sea as he had promised, giving his goddess her due. And aware of her love, he takes Nancy with him. It may seem a strange way of showing love, but clearly this is how Nancy interprets it. When Ethan says that he will not let her accept the blame for what they have done, that they will ''go together,'' she replies with joy, ''Oh, Ethan, you do love me then. I'm so glad.'' Thus, though Ethan has not learned to love, he at least attempts to make Nancy feel loved.

We can only guess what will happen to the remaining three sons. Wolfe, drawn into the card game at last, wins Leda (or she, him; it is not clear which), and thus will become involved in life's drama. We anticipate, given the last title O'Neill settled upon for Wolfe's play, ''The Earth is the Limit,'' that he, too, will come to an unfortunate end. Honey's play, ''Nothing Is Lost but Honor,'' suggests the same; we expect little more from Jonathan.

Thus, had the cycle unfolded, the many variations on the theme of possession-dispossession would have demonstrated again and again the same yearnings and the same disappointments. For instance, that Elizabeth seduces Jonathan and deliberately becomes pregnant to ensure that he will marry her, precisely as Sara had done before her, suggests that nothing is learned from the foibles and failures of previous generations. The cycle echoes scripture: ''the sins of the fathers are visited on the children, even to the third and fourth generation.''

The last instance of time's circularity is associated with the motif of rebirth, mentioned not infrequently in the play. In an already quoted passage, for instance, Ethan tells Sara that if he can defeat the sea, he will be ''reborn.'' Nancy feels that marrying Ethan will allow her to start all over again, and Sara's trip to the West is cast in similar terms. Indeed, the *Dream of the West,* like the American dream, holds forth that very allure for all its passengers.

In *The Calms of Capricorn,* however, the dream lies out there in the inaccessible future. In the present there is no savor of salvation, no agency for spiritual regeneration. The family, which throughout the biographical-historical cycle holds the key to individual reintegration into the community, does not nurture its own members or provide sustenance for the larger network of which it is a part. With the family-business link, the operative mode is competition, gain at the expense of the "other," whoever that might be.

If this meant closing ranks against the outside world, at least competition would promote solidarity within the family. Unfortunately, this does not seem to be the case. The competitive approach quickly filters down to the individual level, so that it becomes a case of each man for himself. This is poignantly illustrated by the play's final sequence. Ethan, agonizing over his crimes and close to suicide, confesses his deeds to Jonathan and Honey. "I murdered the first mate, I murdered the Captain, in order that I might possess life," he cries (*Calms* 115). Jonathan's initial response is telling: "You're a fool. You shouldn't trust even us with such a secret!" The implication is clear; no one can be trusted, not even family, since ultimately each will do what is best for himself. Jonathan, in short, would divulge Ethan's secret if it were to his own advantage, a sad commentary, indeed, on the family's capacity for love. Thus, when Ethan approaches Sara moments later, in a scene which approaches a confession, we are prepared for her response. Ethan insists that Sara judge him and she refuses, saying, "Now go, and God damn the honor of the Harfords!" Ethan is not seeking his mother's forgiveness, nor does he feel the need for absolution; he merely wants her to understand what he is about to do. This play contains no ritual, no hope for transcending time. The drama ends with Sara's tragic cry at her loss: "Ethan! My first-born!"

This play, unlike *Poet* or *Mansions,* does not include a return to origins. Ethan's suicide, a return to "mother sea," is a rebirth only in that he makes his leap in company with Nancy. Then the devouring sea swallows them both. In the last analysis, Ethan's experience offers little hope for his brothers or the generations to come, but for a different set of reasons than those we associate with his cycle relatives. Like Con, Simon, and the characters of the autobiographical plays to come, he is defeated by time, but his experience of it is significantly different. He has defined his fate in terms of the future and sees life in those terms until the end. For him happiness, fulfillment, and peace are within reach; he need only beat the record of the *Flying Cloud* and thus prove his mastery over nature. This presents an important departure from the other historical-biographical plays, where the orientation is primarily toward the past, and the future holds little hope. It also explains why Ethan's romantic quest fires the imagination of the passengers on board his ship. Because his goal is located in the future, and hence is still within the realm of possibility, and because it is mensurable, definite, clear-cut, they latch on to his dream and make it their own.

The qualities of this objective, it is important to note, are nineteenth-century American. Science, technology, progress will master nature with clear-eyed practicality and a predilection for numbers and facts. Faith in progress—every day we are better and better—evokes the hope that defies precise articulation but nonetheless shapes our lives: the American dream. This dream promises that life will be better in the future, for ourselves and, even move important, for our children.

Thus Ethan's struggle contributes to an American ethos O'Neill seems to be shaping in this play. As each generation passes and we move ever further from ethnic roots, the dreams and the dreamers are increasingly American rather than Irish or Yankee. What remains constant is O'Neill's preoccupation with time and its relationship to the potential for achieving happiness, peace, and fulfillment. Americans, as O'Neill sees them, have sought fulfillment through possessions—power and wealth, the love of another person, or one's own fate. The role that time plays in this process varies from play to play, but always the characters must confront it, by dealing with the past, or here, by addressing the future. Variously they discover—or at least *we* do—that there is no possibility for transcending their experience, no regeneration and renewal where possession is the only passion and even love is ownership. In *The Calms of Capricorn* O'Neill presents us with a story of dispossession and despair.

5

The Iceman Cometh and *Hughie:*
Tomorrow Is Yesterday

Harry Hope's saloon in *The Iceman Cometh* is the land that time forgot. A run-down bar and rooming house of the "last resort variety" on the West Side of New York, it is inhabited by a curious collection of misfits and societal outcasts who are living in the past. Appropriately, as the curtain rises, all but two of them are asleep; the atmosphere that prevails for much of the play is one of somnam-bulance, a deathlike calm. In one of the play's oft-quoted passages, Larry Slade, the saloon's elder statesman, explains to a newcomer, Don Parritt, that the "beautiful calm in the atmosphere" stems from the fact that for this dozen-odd human beings, this is the last harbor, the "No Chance Saloon . . . The End of the Line Cafe, The Bottom of the Sea Rathskeller." He adds, "No one here has to worry about where they're going next, because there is no farther they can go."[1] The sea metaphor is apt: The atmosphere in which these men exist is like the half-light that filters to the ocean depths. Dreamlike, deathlike, they live, by common consent, in a world oblivious to clock and calendar—that is, until the drummer Hickey arrives with time's winged chariot at his back. *The Iceman Cometh* is a play about time, both the desire to escape it and the impossibility of doing so.

As we have seen, *Iceman* shares this theme with the earlier cycle plays, *A Touch of the Poet* and *More Stately Mansions.*[2] It recurs in the autobiographical works which will follow: *Hughie, Long Day's Journey,* and *A Moon for the Misbegotten,* all of which, in various ways, focus upon some ideal or lost hope available only to memory. In many ways, *Iceman* stands squarely between these two sets of plays; the pipe-dreaming of this fulcrum play looks both backward to the historical cycle and forward to *Hughie* and the Tyrone saga.

Iceman also occupies a middle position in terms of O'Neill's use of autobiographical material. In his creation of the Melody-Harford family, he drew very obliquely upon his own family members as models. In *Iceman* he turns to his own past more directly for characters and situation, using not his biological family but acquaintances from his Hell Hole, Jimmy-the-Priest days as a young man.[3] His direct use of this autobiographical material seems to have freed him psychologically to tell at last in undisguised fashion the story to which his whole career had been building, that of his own family. *The Iceman Cometh* stands at the crossroad of the historical and biographical cycles, linking them together; the history of its composition reflects the common pathway along which these cycles travelled.[4] For approximately five years before writing *Iceman,* O'Neill's time and energy were consumed in the enormous undertaking of his eleven-play cycle. By the spring of 1939 he had completed first drafts of two of the plays and third drafts of *Poet* and *Mansions,* along with endless notes and outlines for other plays, and was working on *The Calms of Capricorn,* at that time the cycle's fifth play. Then, on June 5, having gone stale on the historical cycle, he decided to put it aside and turn to two plays which he describes in his *Work Diary* as having "nothing to do with" it. These two plays became *The Iceman Cometh* and *Long Day's Journey into Night.* Although he did not recognize it at the time, the two "families" that he limns in these plays are not unrelated to the Melody-Harford clan over which he had been agonizing for the past four-and-one-half years. Both sets of plays, the historical and the autobiographical, actually form a single network, sharing common themes and shaped by a recurring obsession: the need to conquer time. Is it possible, these dramas ask, to escape the bonds of history and move forward, transformed, into a new day, or is Mary Tyrone right when she says that the past is both present and future?

The Iceman Cometh and Linear Time

The action of *Iceman* takes place in 1912, a watershed year in O'Neill's own life (and, not coincidentally, also the time frame he chooses for *Long Day's Journey,* which he outlined in full before turning to the first draft of *Iceman.)*[5] But this is only nominally the era of the play, since all of the boarders at Harry Hope's saloon are living in the past. Larry, we are told, left the anarchist movement eleven years before (1901) and had been involved in it for thirty years (since 1871). Harry hasn't been out of the saloon since his wife Bessie's death twenty years earlier (1892); his favorite song, "She's the Sunshine of Paradise Alley," became popular in 1895. The Boer War, which looms so large in the memories of Piet Wetjoen and Cecil Lewis ("The Captain"), took place in 1899–1902. In fact, about the only specific references to the America of 1912 are the I.W.W. and "du Bull Moosers" in act 1 and the West Coast bombing in which Rosa Parritt was involved.

   The New York that Joe Mott, Harry, and the others recall is that of the 1890s—rich, exciting, and openly corrupt. The framed photographs over the bar are those of Tammany giants Richard Croker and "Big Tim" Sullivan and prize fighters John L. Sullivan and Gentleman Jim Corbett. (The comparison is apt: both Croker and "Big Tim" were known for their prowess with their fists and were fighters in every sense of the word.) Richard Croker, the ruthless Tammany boss from 1886 to 1902, organized corruption on a hitherto unparalleled scale, and Sullivan was in charge of gambling and gambling houses during this era.[6] This is the gilded age when a word from the top and the appropriate payoff were all the insurance necessary. Pat McGloin, Larry tells us, also had his heyday as a police lieutenant "back in the flush times of graft when everything went" (*Iceman* 36).

Even Harry Hope's saloon was a thriving enterprise in the "good old days." "Dis was a first class hang-out for sports in dem days," Joe reminisces. "Good whiskey, fifteen cents, two for two bits" (*Iceman* 46). At that time many aspiring Tammany politicians got their start by running a saloon; hence the talk about running Harry for alderman of the ward. In addition to their individual memories, these characters share a collective nostalgia.

Thus, for this motley crew, the passing of time serves only to mark the increasing distance between the present moment and a past golden age. One of the functions of the paired refrains and stock phrases is to emphasize this point. Their pipe dreams, mutually reinforced, consist in their wan hope that "tomorrow" they will restore the glories of yesterday. Joe Mott will reopen his gambling house, Jimmy will get back his job in the publicity department, the Captain will return to England, and Wetjoen, to the veldt. The list goes on: every one of the boarders clings to a dream that involves the reinstatement of a past status at some point in the future. A possible exception is Larry Slade, whose pipe dream is his insistence that, disillusioned with life, he wants only to die. For him the past represents not an ideal, but its loss. But that, at bottom, is not unlike the dilemma of the others: while they cling to a sense of wholeness and purpose that they link with former life situations, Larry's sense of mourning, disguised as cynical indifference, stems from the fact that he has had to relinquish the political ideology that gave his life meaning. He tells himself that he longs for death, when really he longs for an ideal like the one lost long ago. Even Cora and Chuck are shaped by their histories. They want to get married and move to a farm, but Cora is afraid Chuck will think he was a sap for marrying a prostitute and use that as an excuse to resume his alcoholism. No one, it would seem, can escape the icy fingers of the past; fate becomes simply what has been.

At this point, the function of memory becomes key. If time has betrayed them, so, in a different way, does memory. Although they turn to it for solace in a world grown cold and indifferent, the passing years have distorted the facts and wishful thinking has done the rest, until their memories only vaguely resemble reality. Jimmy has forgotten that his drunkenness drove his wife into the arms of another man, not vice versa, and that he didn't resign, but was fired; Lewis, that he gambled away regiment money; and Wetjoen, that his family and fellow soldiers disowned him for cowardice when he advised Cronje to retreat; none are free to go home. Further, the changes that time has brought have precluded the simple resumption of past positions. New faces have replaced the old ones, contacts are no longer available, jobs have been given to others.

Before Hickey's arrival, however, the bums can hide from these painful truths with the help of two anodynes, booze and a chorus willing to pretend belief in their pipe dreams. The ultimate objective of both these remedies, of course, is to try to stop the clock. The bottom-of-the-sea calm that Larry speaks of stems from this effort to simply repeat the present moment, unchangingly, again and again. This accounts for the endless repetitions that characterize *Iceman*—the stock epithets and repeated phrases associated with virtually all of the characters, the ritualistic recitation of the various pipe dreams, even the endless iterations of the phrase "pipe dream" itself.[7] O'Neill reinforces these repetitions by pairing the characters. Lewis and Wetjoen reenact the Boer War, Mosher and McGloin join forces to wheedle a drink out of Harry, Margie and Pearl tease Rocky. It is clear from the outset that these exchanges have occurred before and will occur again. Their constant repetition has lulled the bums into a sleeplike state where "worst is best . . . and East is West, and tomorrow is yesterday" (*Iceman* 44). Opposites cancel out and time stands still.

The overall action of *Iceman* underscores this cyclic sense of time. Egil Tornqvist is among several critics who have pointed to this fact:

> *Iceman* begins rather harmoniously; the denizens of Hope's saloon have passed out and even after they wake up they contentedly go on pipe-dreaming. With Hickey's entrance it radically changes into the somber bleakness that comes of a life without illusions—and liquor. But once Hickey has been judged insane and has left, back comes the initial mood: the play ends with a cacophonous chorus, indicating that everyone is "just a few drinks ahead of the passing out state." The movement is thus from happy sleep (illusions) through a painful awakening to life's realities and back into happy sleep.[8]

All references to the past are not golden; O'Neill includes historical allusions to civilizations that fell and revolutions that failed—an instance of cyclic time in the classical sense. Hugo, for instance, is fond of referring to Babylon, the luxurious ancient capital of the Chaldean empire which supported its wealth by subjecting the Israelites to slave labor. Babylon is again suggested when Larry describes the birthday party as "a second feast of Belshazzar with Hickey to do the writing on the wall" (*Iceman* 120). The "MENE, MENE, TEKEL, UPHARSIN" of Biblical history foretold the fall of Belshazzar's kingdom to the Medes and the Persians. The world of *Iceman*, it is implied, will also be weighed in the balance and found wanting.

Revolutions seem to promise little improvement in this scheme of things. The anarchist movement in which Larry and Parritt participated led only to bombings. The French Revolution, recalled by "Dansons la Carmagnole" and Lewis' reference to Hugo as "our little Robespierre," resulted in the Reign of Terror. Even the American Revolution, recalled by Parritt's mention of Washington and Jefferson, led in the end to Harry Hope's saloon.

The audience, of course, is acutely conscious that these efforts to escape linear time are doomed to failure. Though constant repetition may dull time's effect, it cannot banish time altogether, a fact which is demonstrated by Hickey's arrival. His message of salvation is threatening to the derelicts precisely because it pierces through to this truth. To achieve peace, he insists, they must give up their pipe dreams and acknowledge that they—and the world—have changed. They must, in short, reenter the world of the present. Hickey has the smell of reality on his breath rather than rot-gut whiskey.

Before the events of these two days, Hickey's relationship with the derelicts had been a part of their yearly cycle. As Larry explains to Parritt, Hickey "comes here twice a year regularly on a periodical drunk" (*Iceman* 24). Participation in these biannual binges helped the boarders as much as Hickey; for the moment, history was abolished, renewing their belief in their respective pipe dreams and reinvesting their experience with reality and value. Thus restored, they could make it "through time" until Hickey arrived again. But from the play's beginning, it is clear that something has changed. Hickey is late, and the cycle has been interrupted. "I wonder what's happened to him," Rocky says. "Yuh could set your watch by his periodicals before dis. Always got here a coupla days before Harry's birthday party, and now he's on'y got till tonight to make it" (*Iceman* 13).

Hickey's conversion , which becomes obvious upon his arrival, can be seen as a function of his newly acquired consciousness of time. As such, he is the only character in the drama associated with linear time. He is, for instance, the timekeeper at Harry's party. He glances down at his watch, timing Harry's entrance for exactly midnight. As Hope appears in the door Hickey looks up and shouts, "On the dot! It's twelve! . . . Come on now, everybody, with a happy birthday, Harry!" (*Iceman* 135). His birthday gift to Harry is a wristwatch, engraved with the date as well as Hope's name. (A more ironic gift to Harry or any of the other boarders is hard to imagine.)[9] Hickey's sense of urgency stems from his consciousness that time is running out. "I had to make you help me with each other," he says. "I saw I couldn't do what I was after alone. Not in the time at my disposal. I knew when I came here I wouldn't be able to stay with you long. I'm slated to leave on a trip" (*Iceman* 147). Having alerted the police to his whereabouts, Hickey is acutely aware that time is running out on his last chance to convert his friends and thereby assuage his own sense of guilt. For unlike the others, Hickey's life has radically changed. His decision to murder his wife, Evelyn, has rendered impossible the pipe dream that he will reform "tomorrow" and all will be well. He is forced to acknowledge present reality, and he desperately wants the others to do likewise.

It is precisely at this juncture that the play employs ritual; actually, two religious rituals, holy communion and confession, both deeply rooted in O'Neill's Catholic upbringing.[10] Religious allusions appear repeatedly throughout the play; the title itself is a cross between the bawdy joke about the iceman "coming" and an allusion to the foolish virgins of Matthew 25:6, who are warned to trim their lamps because "the bridegroom cometh." Hickey, of course, is not the expected bridegroom, a bona fide savior. He is rather the iceman, and the iceman is death, as Larry aptly comments. Hickey is not Christ, but anti-Christ; his salvation offers not fulfillment but annihilation. His actions, then, are the reverse of the Savior's. Christ turned water into wine; Hickey's wine is watered down. "What did you do to the booze, Hickey?" is the constant refrain. "There's no damned life left in it" (*Iceman* 26). Jesus told his disciples, "My peace I give unto you"; Hickey says, "I couldn't give you my peace. You've got to find your own" (*Iceman* 112). Hickey wants to cure his friends, but by stripping away their illusions and sending them out into the sweltering August morning, he merely renders them pathetic and defenseless.

Hickey fails as priest, as well. He would like to hear his friends' confessions, and, indeed, seeks them out individually to do just that. "He's been hoppin' from room to room all night," Rocky complains to Larry. "Yuh can't stop him" (*Iceman* 157). His penance is that they act on their pipe dreams, assuming that, as the dreams failed to materialize, the boarders would be rid of them forever. But his mission is doomed from the outset. The confessions are coerced, not made sincerely as the ritual requires, and his gospel, based on a false premise, is fraudulent. Hickey thinks he wants to save his friends, but actually, he is in need of salvation himself.

Thus, as the play reaches its climax, the real confessions take place and O'Neill's use of ritual becomes more direct. The parallels to Christ's last supper establish the eucharistic ritual as a backdrop to the action of the play, but in Hickey and Parritt's dual confessions we actually see a ritual enacted before our eyes, although it first appears that neither man feels the need of expiating his crime. When, for instance, Parritt confesses to Larry that his motives for betraying his mother weren't patriotic, as he initially insisted, but financial, he seems to feel no remorse for what he has done. The stage directions point out that "he has the terrible grotesque air, in confessing his sordid baseness, of one who gives an excuse which exonerates him from any real guilt" (*Iceman* 160). He has been driven relentlessly, first to find Larry and then to make him his confessor, and he clearly wants Slade to discover his crime, but precisely what sin needs absolution is not yet apparent.

It is the same with Hickey, who for much of the play seems anything but the contrite sinner. His first revelation, that his wife is dead, is spoken in quiet tones. When they gasp, stunned, he quickly reassures them that there is no need for this to spoil Harry's party: "There's no reason—You see, I don't feel any grief. . . . I've got to feel glad, for her sake. Because she's at peace. She's rid of me at last." All this is said with "a simple, gentle frankness" (*Iceman* 151). Even his confession the next day that Evelyn has been murdered is made "quietly" and "matter-of-factly." His only concern at this point is that the peace he has promised Hope and the others is not taking hold. He "gazes with worried kindliness at Hope'' and says, ''You're beginning to worry me, Governor. . . . It's time you began to feel happy—'' (*Iceman* 207). It is only at the end of the second day, when it is clear that Hickey's plan has failed, that his carefully composed facade begins to crumble. His sense of urgency, like Parritt's, reaches a point where a confession clearly must be made.

Both make one last desperate attempt to achieve the peace which has thus far eluded them. In this climactic scene, with Hickey's powerful sustained monologue and Parritt's contrapuntal interjections, both turn to the appropriate parties for forgiveness and understanding: Parritt, to Larry, who, if not his biological father, has come to fulfill that role; Hickey, to Hope and the other boarders, the family he has chosen over his own wife.[11] Parritt has insisted all along that Larry was the only one who could really understand his dilemma—not just because he serves as Don's father, but also because he too has known Rosa's rejection. Hickey instinctively knows he must convince Harry and the others of the necessity of his deed, though he is wrong about his motive. He rationalizes that they, understanding the reason for his peace, will relinquish their own pipe dreams and be equally at rest. Actually, however, he needs them to validate his decision to murder Evelyn, a decision that he has begun to question. Thus their choice of confessors is fitting in terms of the events and relationships of the play.

It is also appropriate in terms of the religious ritual that structures this scene. The Catholic rite of confession is designed to reincorporate the penitent sinner into the mystical body of the church. The priest is efficacious as confessor to the extent that he represents the spiritual community as a whole; this is the source of his power. In the joint confessions of Hickey and Parritt, both priest and community are represented. Larry Slade, who is described at the outset as having a face with ''the quality of a pitying but weary old priest's'' (*Iceman* 5), plays the part of confessor; Harry and his cronies represent the community.[12]

The question, then, becomes whether the confessions take hold. Thus far the efforts of both Parritt and Hickey have failed, since neither has been willing to admit his true sin. They need absolution, not so much for their crimes as for the motives which inspired them. Both have gradually revealed their secrets, one step at a time, throughout the course of the play, and now the moment of truth-telling is at hand. As Hickey tells his story to Hope and the boarders, and Parritt, in antiphonal fashion, echoes the drummer's confession point by point to Larry, we learn that the real sin, which both have refused to acknowledge, is their hatred.

Hickey insists, of course, that this is not the case. As he finally reveals the whole truth about Evelyn's death, he continually reiterates that his only motive was love. His search for ''the one possible way to free poor Evelyn and give her the peace she's always dreamed about,'' he explains to the boarders, was complicated by the great love they felt for each other. The derelicts, however, remain unconvinced, and Hickey, to demonstrate his sincerity, goes back to the beginning. As his story unravels, however, in spite of his protestations to the contrary, Hickey's anger and resentment begin to surface. "If she'd only admitted once she didn't believe any more in her pipe dream that some day I'd behave!" he exclaims (*Iceman* 238). "Sometimes," he goes on, "I couldn't forgive her for forgiving me. I even caught myself hating her for making me hate myself so much" (*Iceman* 239). Thus when he reaches the climax of his confession, still insisting on his love for her, we are not surprised to hear him say: "I remember I stood by the bed and suddenly I had to laugh. I couldn't help it, and I knew Evelyn would forgive me. I remember I heard myself speaking to her, as if it was something I'd always wanted to say: 'Well, you know what you can do with your pipe dream now, you damned bitch!' " (*Iceman* 241).

The ritual has served one purpose; Hickey's true sin has been uncovered. It is his hatred that has driven him to make converts of his friends in order to assuage his own guilt. His anger in the face of Evelyn's pipe dream, his resentment at her attempt to make him over in her own image—these are the furies that have pursued Hickey to this moment of truth. But it is a truth he cannot abide. Rather than confront his deep hatred for Evelyn, he falls back on the comforting delusion of insanity, even when it means allowing Harry and the others to reclaim their own pipe dreams. Thus Hickey is led off in darkness, denying this blinding insight into his soul. The confession has not proved efficacious since Hickey denies what it has taught him.

Parritt, on the other hand, is able to face the truth about himself. Like Hickey, at first he insists that he loved his mother. But gradually the truth unfolds. When Hickey recalls that he tore up Evelyn's picture, Parritt confesses to burning Rosa's. When Hickey admits that he murdered Evelyn, Parritt "suddenly gives up and relaxes limply in his chair," saying "in a low voice in which there is a strange exhausted relief, 'I may as well confess, Larry. There's no use lying any more. You know, anyway. I didn't give a damn about the money. It was because I hated her' " (*Iceman* 241). Interestingly, Parritt's unmasking is completed before Hickey's. While the drummer is still confessing the deed itself, Parritt pierces through to its cause. This is the moment he has been waiting for, the moment of truth.

The crucial difference, however, is that Parritt refuses to deny what he has discovered. "I can't kid myself like Hickey, that she's at peace," he says. "And I'm not putting up any bluff, either, that I was crazy afterwards when I laughed to myself and thought, 'You know what you can do with your freedom pipe dream now, don't you, you damned old bitch!' " (*Iceman* 247). At this, Larry explodes with the judgment Parritt has sought all along: "Go! Get the hell out of life, God damn you, before I choke it out of you!" Parritt's manner, we are told, "is at once transformed. He seems suddenly at peace with himself." As he leaves, about to become his own executioner, his words to Larry are simple and grateful: "Jesus, Larry, thanks. That's kind. I knew you were the only one who could understand my side of it" (*Iceman* 248). Parritt's confession has brought him peace because he accepts the truth it revealed.

The epithet in Parritt's response is no accident, nor is Larry's curse, for the issues in this scene are ultimately spiritual in nature. Both Parritt and Hickey, and, insofar as they are identified with them, the other derelicts, as well, desperately desire the peace which has heretofore evaded them. One way to articulate the nature of their impasse at this point is in terms of time, a concern which unites them all. The past, as we have said, is forever past, and insofar as memory has made of it an Eden (for Parritt, before he betrayed his mother; for Hickey, before he murdered Evelyn; for the others, those periods with dreams still intact or in reach), the present holds only emptiness and the future, only death. They need a means of escaping into another dimension of time, where the virulence of linear time and the futility of cyclic repetition can for the moment be suspended. Thus it seems neither accidental nor insignificant that, at precisely this point, the play draws upon a religious ritual to structure the action. The confessional ritual is a key to the action at this climactic moment, and it is best explained in terms of time and memory.

Ritual, in allowing for the momentary suspension of time, the experience of sacral time, if you will, collapses past, present, and future into a single moment. One is reminded of Yahweh's injunction to Moses to tell the Israelites, held captive in Egypt, that "I am" has sent him. God makes no distinction between past, present, and future; all is subsumed in an eternal now, much like the time frame of Nietzsche's eternal return and Eliade's cosmogonic rituals. Thus, in the presence of faith, the participating believer who can, within the context of ritual, tap the dimension of the divine can experience a moment outside time. It is admittedly a mysterious experience, like all ecstatic or mystical phenomena, one that defies precise articulation and one that is not automatically attained by all participants in religious rituals. Nonetheless, it is the underlying source of power that rituals offer: the intersection of the human with the divine, the family of man transformed into the communion of saints.

Hickey's confession, we have said, proves inefficacious, since he denies the truth it reveals, and Parritt's, though it brings him solace, still exacts the penance of death. Time has run out for them both, though Parritt leaves life strangely renewed, if not forgiven.[13] The boarders still have time left, however, and they embrace this sudden realization with gusto in the play's closing moments. With Parritt and Hickey gone, they return to their pipe dreams, declaring Hickey insane and discovering that the booze has regained its kick. Although this is not sacramental wine they drink, it does derive its power from a communion of sorts, the earthly communion of Harry and his family. And although it does not offer salvation or any kind of ultimate regeneration, it does help them kill time, literally, as they wait for the iceman, death.

Even that solace is denied Larry, who calls himself "Hickey's one true convert." Left alone without even a pipe dream to warm him, Slade has now taken Hickey's place, a fact which is emphasized by Hugo's response to Larry as he listens agonizingly for sounds of Don's suicide. Sitting at Larry's table, Hugo eyes him uneasily and says, "What's matter, Larry? Why you keep eyes shut? You look dead. What you listen for in backyard?" (*Iceman* 254). When Larry, still transfixed, does not answer, he gets up hastily and joins the group around Harry, muttering with frightened anger, "Crazy fool! You vas crazy like Hickey! You give me bad dreams, too" (*Iceman* 254). Larry is now the outsider, watching and waiting, not just for Don's death, but also his own.

Thus the possibility of transcending the limitations of time ultimately fails to materialize. In the confession ritual O'Neill presents a strategy for experiencing the regenerative mythic moment, but it is one that ultimately fails. One cannot live without illusions, the play tells us; "the lie of a pipe dream is what gives life to the whole misbegotten mad lot of us, drunk or sober" (*Iceman* 10).[14]

O'Neill's play, then, refuses to provide a way out for Parritt and Hickey. Their well-hidden hatred is finally revealed and, although they respond differently to it, each must pay with his life. Insofar as both characters are reflections of the playwright's own life experience, this suggests that—at this point, at any rate—O'Neill is unable to resolve his own sense of guilt. The tension that is at the root of so much of his creativity is focused clearly in the fates of Parritt and Hickey. Through them, O'Neill pursues his own relentless search for salvation. It is a search that he will continue in his next play, *Long Day's Journey into Night,* where he will once again employ the confessional ritual to explore the possibility of transcending time.

Hughie

Hughie, O'Neill's one-act play from the *By Way of Obit* series, presents a condensed version of *The Iceman Cometh.*[15] Its themes, concerns, and anagogue replicate those of its longer predecessor; its characters, too, are fighting a losing battle with time.

O'Neill composed *Hughie* at the height of his creative powers. It is, in fact, excepting *A Touch of the Poet* and *A Moon for the Misbegotten,* the last play he was to complete, though he conceived the idea two years earlier. After completing *The Iceman Cometh* on December 20, 1939, referring to it in his *Work Diary* as "one of [the] best plays I've written," O'Neill turned immediately to *Long Day's Journey into Night.* He worked steadily on it from January 1940 through April of the following year, stopping occasionally to jot down notes or outlines for new plays or returning to the historical cycle. During this period, on November 29, 1940, O'Neill conceived *By Way of Obit,* a series of five short, monologue plays. A few days later he added notes for three more, bringing the total to eight.[16]

He outlined scenarios for several of the one-acts, but in the face of his encroaching illness and the prospect of further deterioration, O'Neill destroyed them on February 21, 1944; only *Hughie,* the sole completed play (finished June 23, 1942), was preserved.[17] It appears to be fairly representative of the venture as a whole. According to a letter to drama critic George Jean Nathan in July of 1942, "It [*Hughie*] give [*sic*] you an idea of how the others in the series will be done."[18]

In *Hughie,* O'Neill has created a small gem whose brilliance derives as much from its economy of characterization as from its poetic use of language. Like *Iceman, Hughie* deals with issues of time as well as the need for life-sustaining illusions. The plays thus have much in common. Though the particulars vary, both present a world in decline. *Iceman* focuses its attention on a seedy bar in New York's West Side in 1912; *Hughie,* on a run-down hotel near Times Square in 1928. While fifteen societal dropouts inhabit the world of *The Iceman Cometh,* in *Hughie* there are only two. In both cases, however, we are presented with failed communities. As the boarders at Harry Hope's have formed a family of their own to ward off the desperation that threatens to engulf them, Erie Smith, a small-time gambler, seeks a similar comfort in the companionship of the new night clerk at his hotel, Charlie Hughes. The common denominator in both cases is the need for a pipe dream, since life cannot be endured without a protective shield of illusion. The only obstacle to happiness in this scheme of things arises when someone refuses to play by the rules, challenging the validity of the dream and breaking its soporific spell. For Harry and his crew, this occurs when Hickey arrives, peddling a return to the present. For Smith, the game breaks down with the death of Hughie, the previous night clerk, who participated in his fantasies of excitement and glamour. Erie must find a replacement for his feckless pal, since the dream must be shared to be believed. Around this need the plot, such as it is, unfolds.

Nirvana, the Big Night of Nights

As the action opens, somewhere between 3:00 and 4:00 A.M. on a summer morning in 1928, both Charlie and Erie are losing their respective battles with time. Charlie, in his early forties, has been a night clerk so long, we are told, he has forgotten even how to be bored. His "blank brown eyes contain no discernible expression,"[19] and he has perfected the art of seeming to listen to endless patrons without actually hearing them. His primary objective is to get through the night, to pass the time, which he does by ticking off the various sounds of the city that parcel out the hours. We learn about him primarily through the stage directions, which describe his reactions to these street noises, his inner clock. Early in the play, for instance, as Smith is trying to strike up a conversation with him, the stage directions indicate that the clerk's mind remains in the street. The garbagemen have come and gone, and now he's listening for the El. Its approach is "pleasantly like a memory of hope," but as it roars by, then recedes into the distance it leaves a melancholy echo in the air. But still there is hope, Hughes thinks to himself: "Only so many El trains pass in one night, and each one passing leaves one less to pass, so the night recedes, too, until at last it must die and join all the other long nights in Nirvana, the Big Night of Nights. And that's life" (*Hughie* 19).

This passage sums up nicely Hughes's attitude toward time. He has long since given up hope of attaining meaning in his life, so that the future holds no promise and the present offers only boredom. Unlike the boarders at Harry Hope's, he doesn't even have the memory of a happier past, real or imagined, to warm him. We learn a little about Charlie's past in the course of the play. We know he came from Saginaw, Michigan to New York, ostensibly to make his fortune (like all the other suckers, Erie comments cynically). He is married and has three children, the oldest of whom is eleven, or maybe twelve, he can't remember. For all intents and purposes, emotionally and psychologically (and spiritually, one might add), Charlie died a long time ago. He has learned not to react to the predictable wisecracks of the endless, anonymous hotel guests ("That's what comes of being careless," Erie says of the clerk's three children) and can scarcely recall feeling any emotions at all. The last time he was able to feel despair, we are told, was when he was out of a job for three months some fifteen years ago.

His experience of time combines linear and cyclic modes. To kill time, he ticks off the night sounds: the garbagemen, the El, the cop on his beat. After years of experience, these have become as carefully calibrated as any clock; he doesn't need to consult the one hanging on the wall. Yet as each night joins the next, the overall effect is cyclic since, sooner or later, all nights must end. The nirvana he experiences now, a kind of mindless oblivion, is a precursor of the death he longs for. When he hears the ambulance in the street and imagines a conversation with the attending physician, he says, "Will he die, Doctor, or isn't he lucky?" (*Hughie* 26). It is no accident that he shares the name of a dead man.

Erie Smith, down on his luck and nearing desperation, is also associated with both modalities of time in the play. Like Charlie, he takes comfort in the cyclic nature of experience. He's hit losing streaks before, he tells the clerk, but he always bounces back; life has its ups and downs. "I've been in the big bucks," he says. "More'n once, and I will be again" (*Hughie* 15). This faith, we suspect, has helped him to survive.

Furthermore, the play implies that his experience is fairly typical. O'Neill assigns him the name "Smith" quite deliberately, then draws our attention to it by having Erie emphasize that it's his real name ("Ain't that a knockout!").

He insists that Charlie call him "Erie," since if there's a sucker (and a night clerk) born every minute, he says, there are *ten* Smiths born during the same time, thousands of "Smiths" following the same cycle.

Erie is also associated with time as a continuum: one way, irreversible, and in his case—as in so many of O'Neill's characters of this period—downward. Even allowing for his tendency to exaggerate in his own favor (he is described in the list of characters as a teller of tales), we gather that life for Smith has been a steady, if gradual, decline. He tells of meeting Hughie for the first time just after returning from Tijuana where he'd made a "big killing." He returned all the way in a drawing room with a blond movie star. "I was lucky in them days," he says. "Used to follow the horses South every winter," he adds, but "I don't no more. Sick of traveling" (*Hughie* 23). He insists, arousing our suspicions, that he can still "make" the Follies dolls if he wants to; "I ain't slippin' " (*Hughie* 16). The hourglass keeps emptying, and even Erie can't deny it completely.

In some ways, he doesn't want to. Like Hickey before him, Erie is an apostle of change. What Hughie needed in his life was "interest," Erie insists. In the fantasies that the gambler would spin for the dead clerk, stories of glamour and excitement, horse racing and fancy cars and beautiful women (in that order), he brought vitality and zest to the dull routine of Hughie's life, one much like that of the present clerk. In this, he reminds us of the early Hickey, who, before the events of *Iceman*, used to join the bums in a binge twice yearly, blowing in like a breath of fresh air and relieving the stultifying boredom of their lives.[20] Like another predecessor, Con Melody, Erie relied on his imagination to create a persona that Hughie would find exciting. "The bigger I made myself the more he lapped it up," Erie says. "He thought gangsters was romantic. So I fed him some baloney about highjacking I'd done once. I told him I knew all the Big Shots. . . . Hughie wanted to think me and Legs Diamond was old pals. So I give him that too. I give him anything he cried for" (*Hughie* 28–29).

The difference between this self-creation and that of Con (aside from the fact that Con's is more solidly anchored in reality) is that Erie's tale-telling depends upon an audience. Melody bolsters his self-esteem in front of a mirror; he speaks only to himself, while Smith's self-creation, like the pipe dreams of Harry and company, is communitarian in nature.

Erie has managed to survive thus far by virtue of his relationship with Hughie. His nightly return to an admiring audience imposed some sense of meaning or purpose on the trivial events of the day. "Some nights I'd come back here without a buck, feeling lower than a snake's belly," he tells Charlie, "and first thing you know I'd be lousy with jack, bettin' a grand a race. Oh, I was wise I was kiddin' myself. I ain't a sap. But what the hell, Hughie loved it, and it didn't cost nobody nothin', and if every guy along Broadway who kids himself was to drop dead there wouldn't be nobody left" (*Hughie* 29). This is basically a cyclic experience of life. The mutual pipe dreams of the night give both men the strength to face the coming day. But reality intrudes with Hughies's death, and Erie's luck and confidence abruptly disappear. Time has caught up with him.

Charlie, too, is defeated by the passage of time. The usual comfort he derives from the routines of the night, the El trains and streetcars passing into oblivion one by one, is suddenly not enough. As he counts the slow hours, we are aware that his real battle is not with this guest who won't stop talking or his aching feet or even his humdrum existence, but with time itself. Director Bengt Ekerot of Stockholm's Royal Dramatic Theatre reflected this dimension when, at the play's world premiere, he had the clerk count silently on his fingers as each El train passed—a gesture which reviewer Henry Hewes called "the action most essential to the drama."[21]

At Erie's lowest point, when he is "too defeated even to twirl his room key" (*Hughie* 30), the symbolic fetish with which he wards off death,[22] Charlie also reaches his nadir. The stillness of the night closes in on him and reminds him of life's final silence, death: "The Clerk's mind still cannot make a getaway because the city remains silent, and the night vaguely reminds him of death . . . 'I should have paid 492 more attention. After all, he is company. He is awake and alive. I should use him to help me live through the night.' " (*Hughie* 30). Thus he seizes upon Erie in the hope that his rambling chatter will bring him back to life. He recalls Smith's mention of gambling, and, as it occurs to him that Erie might know his hero, Arnold Rothstein, he "is now suddenly impervious to the threat of Night and Silence" (*Hughie* 32). The link between the two lonely, desperate men is forged and, as Charlie assumes the role of the dead clerk, the old cycle is once again resumed. If linear time has not been defeated, they have at least discovered a way to cheat it a little longer.

As such, the play ends on a positive note; life wins out over death, although it is hardly what one would call optimistic.[23] It is true that life prevails—at least for the moment, and that a bond is formed between two human beings that will strengthen and sustain them both. But the vision of life that O'Neill presents to us is attenuated at best. There is no possibility of transcendence, no viable means of breaking through the limitations of time and space, no discovery of ultimate meaning or value. O'Neill employs religious language at the point of the clerk's transformation ("Beatific vision swoons on the empty pools of [his] eyes. He resembles a holy saint, recently elected to Paradise"), but the images echo ironically. The "rapt hero worship [which] transfigure[s] his pimply face" (*Hughie* 32) is merely for Arnold Rothstein, a gambler associated with the New York underworld as well as Tammany Hall, hence a symbol of the city's corruption. The cycle of mutual self-deception is merely perpetuated, as Charlie takes Hughie's place and the pipe dream goes on.

It is interesting that O'Neill does not employ ritual in this play and that the few religious allusions that he selects are used ironically, especially when we consider the time of *Hughie*'s composition. O'Neill conceived the play as early as 1940 and worked on it intermittently through 1941 and 1942; the last notation of his "going over" this drama, as he puts it in his notebook, occurs in June of 1942. During this period he completed *Long Day's Journey into Night* and a first draft of *A Moon for the Misbegotten,* works in which, as chapters 5 and 6 will detail, O'Neill employs ritual precisely at that juncture when linear time and memory threaten to overwhelm the characters. This would suggest that there is no unwavering, tidy progression in O'Neill's thinking or, in psychological terms, in the resolution of his anguish over personal memories. While he composed the serene *Moon,* a play which puts to rest his dead brother Jamie (and by extension, deals with his own guilt), he worked on the much more cynical *Hughie.* But the central issues in all of the plays remain constant; the themes that obsessed O'Neill throughout the historical cycle continued to haunt him up through his final works. They are questions of the greatest import, dealing ultimately with free will in the face of the past and the prospect of the future, which only brings death with certainty. What are we to do if we live *By Way of Obit?*

6

Long Day's Journey into Night: Descent into Darkness

George Cram Cook, a close friend of O'Neill, once remarked upon the playwright's frequent habit of gazing at himself in the mirror: "You're the most conceited man I've ever known, you're always looking at yourself." "No," O'Neill replied, "I just want to be sure I'm here."[1] To some extent, all of O'Neill's dramas are mirrors that reflect the protean playwright. The clearest image is found in the directly autobiographical *Long Day's Journey into Night,* a play of "old sorrow, written in tears and blood" (*LDJ* dedication). Among the last plays he would complete, it was the play he had been preparing to write from the beginning of his career.

As he composed *Long Day's Journey,* coming to terms with his present by confronting the past, O'Neill once again examined the critical questions that so obsessed him in this phase of his career. The search, now quite directly drawing upon memories of his father, mother, and brother Jamie, all long dead, led him back in time; in composing this play, O'Neill, like so many of his characters from this period, returned to his origins.[2]

Journey into Night

The title of this play suggests from the outset the importance of time. The action, which chronicles a single day in the Tyrone family from morning to midnight, traces in linear fashion its inexorable descent into darkness. The linear aspect of this experience is emphasized in various ways. One obvious instance is the appearance of the fog, which has dispersed with the new morning but gradually sets in again as the day wears on and thickens to an impenetrable blanket by night. The morning sunshine becomes a "faint haziness" (act 2.1) by lunch, increasingly dense by early afternoon (act 2.2), and a thick fog by evening, resembling "a white curtain drawn outside the windows" (act 3). By midnight, we're told, the "wall of fog appears denser than ever" (act 4).

The characters' reaction to the fog is as noteworthy as the fog itself. Early in the play Mary Tyrone, the mother of Jamie and Edmund, who have joined their parents for the summer at the family's seaside cottage, mentions that she didn't sleep well because of the moaning of the foghorn; she is relieved that the fog has lifted. Her attitude, however, changes along with the weather. Though at first she finds the fog dreary and depressing, she begins to welcome it as a place to hide, as does Edmund, who declares in act 4 that the fog was where he wanted to be.

This introduces another chronology in the play. As the action unfolds it quickly becomes obvious that something has happened in the past that haunts the Tyrones and has shaped both their individual experiences of life and their relationships to one another. This knowledge is communicated indirectly at first, chiefly by the discrepancy between what seem to be insignificant pleasantries and banter and the paranoid way in which the characters react during these exchanges. When Mary teases her husband James about his snoring early in act 1, for instance, Jamie quickly picks up on the fact that she couldn't sleep and spent the night in the spare room. At his "uneasy, probing look" Mary becomes anxious and asks him, "Why are you staring, Jamie? Is my hair coming down? It's hard for me to do it up properly now. My eyes are getting so bad and I never can find my glasses." At this, Jamie looks away guiltily and says, "Your hair's all right, Mama. I was only thinking how well you look" (*LDJ* 20).[3] What, we wonder, are they hiding?

This question piques our curiosity and holds our attention as the action unfolds; the first time we read or view the play we tend to focus on the unraveling of this mystery. The clues are revealed gradually, so that it is only in act 3 that we discover with certainty what we have suspected for some time, that Mary is a dope addict. She has just resumed her habit after an abstinence of two months, a development that decimates the family's fragile hopes and dreams. Thus, though earlier Mary complains bitterly about her loneliness and the fact that she has no friends, toward evening she welcomes the obscurity that the fog provides, cutting the Tyrones' cottage off from the rest of the town and isolating them from curious eyes. Edmund, too, seems relieved that he can lose himself in the fog; the phrase is apt.

Both of these linear movements in the play, like that of morning to night, underline the irreversible nature of this mode of time. The fog steadily thickens; Mary's past cannot be escaped.[4] It haunts her unrelentingly, the play suggests, until she finally breaks down and succumbs to the morphine. Though at some point both Edmund and James try to persuade her to stop before it's too late, the action of the play makes it clear that this is not a viable possibility—only what O'Neill was fond of calling a "hopeless hope." It was already too late when she first became addicted. Mary herself puts it most succinctly. "The past is the present, isn't it?" she says. "It's the future, too. We all try to lie out of that but life won't let us" (*LDJ* 87).[5]

The inescapability of past influences is further emphasized by three related developments in the play: Mary's regression into the past, the changes in her physical appearance, and the fragmentation of the family that results from her transformation.

Mary takes morphine again, the play suggests, because of her anxiety over the likelihood that her favorite son Edmund has contracted consumption, a disease which at that time was nearly always fatal, and which killed her father.[6] To escape the pain that this fear brings, a pain she cannot bear, Mary withdraws, via the morphine, into a happier past. Robert C. Lee points out that Mary moves steadily, by stages, in this direction. He writes: [Mary] "retreats in memory from the unmanageable present (1) to the history of her unhappy married life (2) to Edmund's painful birth and her introduction to drugs (3) to Eugene's tragic death (4) to her courtship with James Tyrone (5) to her pious convent days."[7]

Mary's increasingly disheveled appearance parallels this disintegration. As the play begins she is dressed simply but elegantly, her hair is arranged "with fastidious care," and her voice is "soft and attractive" (*LDJ* 13). By lunchtime, having taken a shot of the "poison," as James calls it, her eyes have become brighter and a peculiar detachment has crept into her voice and manner. By dinner, Mary is paler and more detached than before. She wears a simple, fairly expensive dress "which would be extremely becoming if it were not for the careless, almost slovenly way she wears it. Her hair is no longer fastidiously in place. It has a slightly disheveled, lopsided look" (*LDJ* 97). By the play's final scene, Mary's regression is complete. Her face now appears youthful, "a marble mask of girlish innocence" (*LDJ* 170). The elegant dress of act 1 is replaced by a sky-blue dressing gown worn over her nightdress; the painstakingly coiffed hair is now in pigtails. She is paler than ever, and her eyes, now enormous, "glisten like polished black jewels" (*LDJ* 170). Draped carelessly over one arm, her white satin wedding gown trails along behind. The morphine has served its purpose; Mary has escaped the pain of her present by retreating into the innocence of her past.

This retreat, in turn, leads to and parallels the third development mentioned earlier, the increasing isolation of the individual family members and the disintegration of the family unit. When we first meet the Tyrones they seem an affectionate, cohesive family. Although the seeds of dissension are buried just below the surface, as Edmund regales the others with a tale about Tyrone's shiftless tenant Shaughnessy and his taunting of Harker, the Standard Oil millionaire, they momentarily share the camaraderie and *esprit de corps* of the "insider" (i.e., the Irish) against the "outsider" (the Yankee).

From this moment forward, the play begins to move toward the final disintegration of the family. This movement is reflected in the symbolic arrangements O'Neill has prescribed for each of the three family meals, events that mark the passing of time. As the curtain rises, the family has just finished breakfast. Tyrone and Mary enter the living room together, his arm around her waist, and he gives her a playful hug. Soon joined by Jamie and Edmund, the family unites in laughter over Shaughnessy's "great Irish victory" (*LDJ* 25).

Within a few short hours, this happy scene undergoes a drastic transformation. Mary has given way to the temptation of morphine, a fact which has become obvious to her husband and sons. Although the family remains together physically, each member responds to Mary's relapse by withdrawing silently from the others. Tyrone "lights a cigar and goes to the screen door, staring out," Jamie fills a pipe and goes to look out the window at right, and Edmund "sits in a chair by the table, turned half away from his mother so he does not have to watch her" (*LDJ* 71).

By dinnertime, even the pretense of unity has gone by the board. Neither Jamie nor Edmund has returned for supper, and Mary uses the pain in her hands as an excuse to go upstairs and "rest." As she moves off through the front parlor, James "stands a second as if not knowing what to do. He is a sad, bewildered, broken old man. He walks wearily off through the back parlor toward the dining room" (*LDJ* 123). Their final reunion at the end of act 4, when Mary, trancelike, rejoins the men at midnight, becomes a mockery of the closeness suggested by the opening scene.

These linear features of the play are subtly reinforced by a strategy similar to one already encountered in both *A Touch of the Poet* and *More Stately Mansions,* having to do with patterns of cultural assimilation. O'Neill, as has been frequently observed (most notably by critics like Raleigh and Chothia), is extremely accurate in his depiction of cultures and dialects, which in his late plays are primarily Irish and New England Yankee. *Long Day's Journey into Night* is no exception. The Tyrones, their maid Cathleen, and even the neighbor Shaughnessy tell the story of Irish immigrants in America. While this is interesting in and of itself, as we regard the characters not just as individuals, but also as representative stages of assimilation into the American mainstream, we see still another instance of the impact of linear time.

As is so often the case, the first generation immigrant (here, James Tyrone) remains proud of his heritage and recalls the "old country" with fondness, while subsequent generations typically renounce the old customs and strive for complete integration into the new society. Thus, when Jamie berates his father for his "Irish bog-trotter idea" that consumption is fatal, Tyrone snaps back,

> I have every hope Edmund will be cured. And keep your dirty tongue off Ireland! You're a fine one to sneer, with the map of it on your face!
> *Jamie:* Not after I wash my face. (*LDJ* 80)

The exchange is typical (and, like many in the play, is taken from real life).[8]

The various generations' response to their Irish heritage can also be observed in their language. Cathleen represents the Irish immigrant fresh from the shores of the old country. Described as a "buxom Irish peasant . . . with a red-cheeked comely face, black hair and blue eyes," she is "amiable, ignorant, clumsy" (*LDJ* 51). Supplied with a generous stock of Irish aphorisms and superstitions, she has a ready response for all situations. At Mary's mention of fog, Cathleen notes, "They say it's good for the complexion" (*LDJ* 98); a reference to James' snoring brings, "Ah, sure, everybody healthy snores. It's a sign of sanity, they say" (*LDJ* 99). The foghorn reminds her of a banshee;[9] "bad cess to it," she adds (*LDJ* 98). Her attitude toward alcohol is also typically Irish. Like Bridget, Cathleen "loves her drop." She views Tyrone's drinking as "a good man's failing," insisting that she "wouldn't give a trauneen for a teetotaler. They've no high spirits" (*LDJ* 101). Yet—also typically Gaelic—she can just as easily become primly virtuous, as she does when she tells Edmund, "I'd never suggest a man or a woman touch drink, Mister Edmund. Sure, didn't it kill an uncle of mine in the old country" (*LDJ* 52). Cathleen, then, represents the untutored peasant, complete with Irish brogue, syntax, and lexicon.

The next level of assimilation is represented by James, a first-generation immigrant. To succeed as a Shakespearean actor, we are told, he got rid of an Irish brogue so thick "you could cut [it] with a knife" (*LDJ* 150). Although he has left his brogue behind, he still lapses into an occasional Irish phrase or cadence. Early in act 1 he compliments Mary "with Irish blarney" (*LDJ* 28); upon hearing Jamie's late arrival in act 4, he scowls, "That loafer! He caught the last car, bad luck to it" (*LDJ* 154).

All Irish traces have disappeared from the speech of Mary, a second-generation immigrant, though she still sometimes laughs with an "Irish lilt" (*LDJ* 28). Jamie, on the other hand, has not only erased all Irish elements from his speech; he has replaced them with a peculiarly American speech pattern—the patois of Broadway. This is decried not only by Tyrone, but by Edmund as well, representing still another sociological, if not biological, generation. When, for example, Jamie responds cynically to Mary's relapse into addiction, Edmund "scornfully parod[ies] his brother's cynicism": "They never come back! Everything is in the bag! It's all a frame-up! We're all fall guys and suckers and we can't beat the game!" (*LDJ* 76). Their altercation is broken up by James, who responds,

> Shut up, both of you! There's little choice between the philosophy you learned from Broadway loafers, and the one Edmund got from his books. They're both rotten to the core. You've both flouted the faith you were born and brought up in—the one true faith of the Catholic Church—and your denial has brought nothing but self-destruction! (*LDJ* 77)

The profile of each generation emerges in sharp relief: James relies on "the one true faith of the Catholic Church"; Jamie substitutes the lifestyle of Broadway, with its American values of money and fame and flashy clothes; Edmund turns to philosophy and literature, to Nietzsche and the Decadents.

Even the pattern of literary allusions documents their differences. James, the traditionalist, quotes only Shakespeare (who, of course, was an "Irish Catholic"). Jamie, next in line, mixes allusions to Shakespeare with references to the Decadents—Swinburne, Rossetti, Wilde; whatever the source, his quotations are used as weapons against his father. While Tyrone's Shakespearean quotations are primarily moralistic aphorisms ("The fault, dear Brutus, is not in our stars, but in ourselves that we are underlings"), Jamie's are either sarcastic ("The Moor, I know his trumpet," he says of Tyrone's snoring) or cruel ("The Mad Scene. Enter Ophelia!"). Twice he quotes the villainous Iago. He is not of Tyrone's generation; as a "modern," Jamie has his own taste in literature (e.g., the Decadents). However, his use of Shakespeare suggests that he has not completely broken away from his father's influence, although he turns Tyrone's own tradition against him. Edmund, representing still another generation, quotes only Nietzsche, whom Jamie has not read, and the Decadents.[10] Thus each character in *Long Day's Journey* functions simultaneously as an individual and the representative of a different generation, though of course, literally, there are only three immigrant generations in the play.[11]

This insistence upon linear time—seen variously in the steadily encroaching fog, Mary's regression into the past and physical deterioration, the breakdown of the family unit, and the pattern of cultural assimilation that emphasizes the passing of successive generations—makes sense when we understand that each of the Tyrones locates either some ideal or lost ideal in the past. Thus, the moving hand becomes their arch enemy, as it distances them from that moment of peace, happiness, and integration.

These ideal moments, in which opposites were cancelled out and everything seemed possible, are revealed in act 4 as the play builds to its climax. For James, life reached its apex in 1874 when Edmund Booth, the great Shakespearean actor, said to the stage manger of Tyrone's acting, "That young man is playing Othello better that I ever did!" (*LDJ* 150). At that point, James tells Edmund in his midnight confession, "I had life where I wanted it!" The crest of his happiness included Mary: "Her love was an added incentive to ambition," he says. For a brief period he was able to integrate his profession and his family life, opposites that would never be reconciled again. Shortly thereafter he was corrupted by the easy money and sure success of *The Count of Monte Cristo.*"[12] "What the hell was it I wanted to buy," he wonders, "that was worth—Well, no matter. It's a late day for regrets" (*LDJ* 150). But of course, regrets and memories are all that are left him.

Jamie's moment is not that of an ideal realized, but of one lost. Just before his confession to Edmund, he describes the time he discovered his mother "in the act with a hypo." Before that, he says, he "never dreamed any women but whores took dope!" (*LDJ* 163). His discovery changes his entire perspective on life, and he longs to return to his former innocence. This helps explain why it is so desperately important to Jamie that Mary "beat the game." If she can remain abstemious, he can once again believe in her innocence—and hence, in his own: "I'd begun to hope, if she'd beaten the game, I could, too" (*LDJ* 162), he says.

Mary associates her ideal moment with the day of her wedding. At that moment opposites were reconciled and dreams were within reach. But it is an experience that can never be repeated. Her attempts to recreate this past can only be accomplished by totally divorcing herself from reality and disappearing into a morphine fog, at disastrous cost to her family. The culmination of act 4—in fact, of the entire play—is Mary's reunion with the family around the living room table, an ironic parody of the happy scene which began their long journey. Throughout the play, Mary has been looking for something she has lost. Although this is imaged in her lost glasses (she cannot see herself accurately), she is actually searching for her lost innocence, associated with her convent days and her desire to be a nun. Yet in an equally real sense, Mary finds fulfillment and joy in her role as mother. "She was never made to renounce the world," Tyrone tells Edmund. "She was bursting with health and high spirits and the love of loving" (*LDJ* 138). Both needs coalesce in the figure of the Virgin Mother. In the final scene, Mary is wearing a sky-blue dressing gown, a color associated with the Blessed Virgin. Her braids imply her youthful innocence; her wedding gown suggests her potential motherhood—and even recalls the security she associates with her father, who would spare no expense to make her happy. All her desires converge in this moment.

Edmund's ideal is also embodied in an experience which he tries to recapture, but one which differs significantly from that of the others. The ideals of his parents and older brother have both individual and familial components. James's includes fame as a Shakespearean actor and contentment as a husband, Mary's is a wish for chastity and motherhood, and Jamie's combines a desire for self-sufficiency (i.e., independence from his alcoholism) with a dependent, childlike relationship with his mother. All three, of course, are irresolvably contradictory.

Edmund's ideal, on the other hand, does not include the family as a whole or depend upon any of its members individually. The moments of transcendence that he experiences take place when he is alone with the sea—once on the bowsprit of a square rigger late at night, once in the crow's nest during a dawn watch, other times while swimming or lying alone on the beach. Indeed, it is the vicious cycle of family disintegration that drives him out onto the beach in the first place. The familial component, then, is clearly missing in his ideal. For the essence of these moments is a merging with the elements, a phenomenon he describes in this celebrated passage:

> I became drunk with the beauty and singing rhythm of it [the sea], and for a moment I lost myself—actually lost my life. I was set free! I dissolved in the sea, became white sails and flying

spray, became beauty and rhythm, became moonlight and the ship and the high dim-starred sky! I belonged, without past or future, within peace and unity and a wild joy, within something greater than my own life, or the life of Man, to Life itself! To God, if you want to put it that way. (*LDJ* 153)

Unable to experience unity with his family, Edmund seeks union with the cosmos.[13]

Another significant difference is that Edmund's ideal moments can be repeated. Unlike the ideals of the other Tyrones, which are experienced at a specific point in the past and are therefore irretrievable, Edmund's transcendent moments seem to hold out hope for the future, since they are repeatable. This potential, however, is ironically mocked by Edmund's consumption, which threatens to rob him of life itself. Thus for Edmund, too, time is the enemy.

Although the specific components of these ideals differ for each of the characters, for both Mary and James, the high point of life is forever past; each new day serves only to remove them ever further from their ideals. For Jamie, lost innocence also resides in the past. Edmund seems capable of reexperiencing his ideal moments with nature, but the hourglass is emptying; his time is running out.

Memory: A Return to the Past

As memory lures these characters back into the past in an effort to return to their beginnings, to reexperience paradise lost, time turns on itself and becomes cyclic, and their constant awareness of the past takes another shape. Suffering intensely from the vague, nameless guilt associated with their lost ideals,[14] they lash out at each other in an endless round of guilt-accusation-remorse-forgiveness-and counterattack. Nearly every incident of the play provides an instance of this pattern.[15] An altercation between Tyrone and Jamie is typical. At first, Tyrone is defensive about sending Edmund to Dr. Hardy. Then he attacks Edmund for "deliberately ruin[ing] his health by the mad life he's led ever since he was fired from college." When he adds, "Now it's too late," Jamie jumps on his father's "bog-trotter" ideas about consumption. Tyrone counterattacks, alleging that Jamie's adverse influence on Edmund is the real cause of his illness. Now it is Jamie's turn to be defensive. He admits he "did put Edmund wise to things, " but suddenly becomes indignant and insists that he loves Edmund and would do anything for him. Tyrone in turn is mollified and retracts his accusation, but soon the cycle recurs, this time with Tyrone attacking Jamie's "Broadway and bourbon" lifestyle. It is painfully obvious that these same battles have been waged before and will be fought again.

The pattern is so deeply ingrained that they can even anticipate each other's lines. When Tyrone gives Edmund ten dollars for carfare and Edmund is temporarily at a loss for words, James says, "How sharper than a serpent's tooth

it is—!'' and Edmund replies, " 'To have a thankless child.' I know. Give me
a chance, Papa. I'm knocked speechless'' (*LDJ* 89). Later, when Tyrone quotes
Lear's ''Ingratitude, the vilest weed that grows!'' Jamie responds, ''I could see
that line coming! God, how many thousand times—!'' (*LDJ* 32–33). Yet he is
guilty of the same kind of repetition. When Jamie refers to Tyrone as ''Old
Gaspard,'' Edmund snaps irritably, ''Oh, shut up, will you. I've heard that
Gaspard stuff a million times'' (*LDJ* 158).

To reinforce the impact of this repetitious, interchangeable dialogue, O'Neill
puts nearly identical lines in the mouths of different characters. Late at night,
for instance, mulling over Tyrone's crimes against Mary, Edmund says to his
father, ''Jesus, when I think of it I hate your guts!'' (*LDJ* 141). Minutes later,
Jamie says the same thing to Edmund.

The Tyrones don't even need each other to carry on an argument; each is
so consumed by guilt that he can play both parts. When Tyrone praises Edmund's
success as a reporter, for instance, Jamie's jealous response is typical:

> A hick town rag! Whatever bull they hand you, they tell me he's a pretty bum reporter. If he
> weren't your son—
> > *Ashamed again.*
> No, that's not true! They're glad to have him, but it's the special stuff that gets him by. Some
> of the poems and parodies he's written are damned good.
> > *Grudgingly again.*
> Not that they'd ever get him anywhere on the big time.
> > *Hastily*
> But he's certainly made a damned good start. (*LDJ* 36)[16]

These interactions recur because none of the Tyrones can respond to the present
moment *per se*. The present always includes all the pressure of the past. To a
certain extent, of course, that is true for everyone; from this perspective no individual moment is really totally new. Because for the Tyrones the good is defined by something irretrievable, however, no present experience can ever be
fully satisfactory. Thus they not only react in terms of past grudges, betrayals,
and suspicions; they try—albeit unknowingly—to escape present guilt by finding
a scapegoat (the accusational cycles) or, as in act 4, an answer to what went wrong.

This sets up a downward spiral, since movement away from the ideal can
only serve to intensify individual pain and isolation as they lash out at one another
in accusation and counteraccusation. The relationship of morning to night and
clear skies to fog parallels this movement and compounds its implications.
Although the movement of day to night suggests a linear paradigm, we know
that the night will produce yet another morning; so also, with the fog and sunny
skies. Neither travelling forward in time nor circling back via memory, in the
last analysis, will make a significant difference.

Paradise Lost: Confession as Escape from Time

Throughout the play the downward spiral carries the Tyrones through steadily expanding cycles of guilt. As morning advances toward night, the accusations grow increasingly bitter. The passing of time simply intensifies these effects, and, with the exception of Mary's temporary anodyne, all efforts to escape by retreating into the past are doomed to failure.

The same movement structures *Mourning Becomes Electra,* the trilogy which O'Neill patterned on the *Oresteia.* As the Mannons endure the tragic consequences of the family curse, the cycle of love, infidelity, and murder repeats itself with each generation. The play ends with Orin Mannon's suicide and his sister Lavinia's self-immolation in the family manor, "living alone . . . with the dead . . . until the curse is paid out."[17] In *Mourning* O'Neill traces the consequences of guilt to its final desperate conclusion; there are no outs.

Long Day's Journey, however, entertains an alternative to the grim anagogue of the earlier play. While acts 1 through 3, which reveal a situation as guilt-ridden and hopeless as that of the Mannons, seem to be heading toward a similar conclusion, with act 4 the pattern changes, suggesting for the first time the possibility of hope. That this act is substantively different from the previous three is evident in the fact that for the first time, the characters are able to get beyond their deeply ingrained patterns of attack and counterattack and actually communicate with one another. James reveals his long-lost dream of being a great Shakespearean actor and his disillusionment with his misspent life, Edmund tries to explain his mystical experiences at sea, Jamie reveals his deep-seated ambivalence toward his younger brother and his despair at discovering his mother's addiction. The astonishing thing about all this is that they actually listen to one another and that this listening allows new insights. For the first time in the play, new ground is broken, suggesting that perhaps the tyranny of the past can at last be challenged, even overcome.

Again, this potential breakthrough is presented in a ritual. With the confessions mentioned above, new insights and potentially, at least, fresh beginnings seem within reach. Thus, after Tyrone admits that his artistic ambitions were corrupted by his desire for financial security, Edmund, we are told, is "moved" and "stares at his father with understanding." "I'm glad you've told me this, Papa," he says. "I know you a lot better now" (*LDJ* 151). Jamie's confession is equally revealing, as he admits his long-standing jealousy and even hatred of his younger brother. "Gone to confession," he drunkenly concludes. "Know you absolve me, don't you, Kid?" (*LDJ* 167). Morphine has taken Mary to a stage of childhood innocence that precludes the need for a formal confession, but her final speech performs the same function by allowing us to understand her lost ideal and her corresponding sense of guilt.

The Tyrones' willingness to at last confess their own guilt instead of merely accusing one another seems to hold out hope that the cycle of recrimination can be broken. This is, as we have seen, precisely the function of ritual—to allow the participant to begin life anew. Confessing one's sins to a representative of God who is authorized to wipe the slate clean and reestablish harmony with the cosmos is a ritual that, for the believer, recapitulates Christ's mediation between God and man. The past, present, and future of both the individual and humanity at large are thus contained in this reconciliation of the human and the divine. Further, both linear and cyclic modalities of time are operative in that the participant realizes that in spite of the sincerity of his/her confession, at some future point in time (the linear dimension) s/he will again need absolution and the ritual will be repeated (the cyclic modality). It is also important to note that confession includes both individual and communal dimensions. As the sins of the individual are forgiven, he or she is reunited with the Christian community, the family of believers.

This accounts for the stirrings of hope we feel during the events of act 4. As first James and then Jamie make their confessions to Edmund, revealing their lost dreams and the sense of diminishment they have experienced since that loss (complicated for Jamie by his jealousy of Edmund, which he also confesses), we begin to hope that the insights these revelations make available will lead to a renewed unity among the Tyrones. But with Mary's final entrance, a symbolic revelation, as we have said, of her lost ideal, it is clear that the confessional ritual has failed. As the curtain rings down, the Tyrones remain locked in time; nothing has changed.

The ritual's redemptive potential is not realized for at least two reasons. In the first place, Edmund, who serves as the principal confessor, does not qualify as priest. According to Catholic doctrine, the priest as healer and "ministering spirit" (Hebrews 1:14) must first belong to the community himself. He can only act for the Christian family as one of its members, equally in need of the ritual's healing process. But unlike the other Tyrones, whose ideals all include both individual and familial components, Edmund's ideal is exclusively individual. His transcendental moments can only be experienced when he is alone with nature. In fact, insofar as they require an abdication of individuality, they actually represent a kind of death wish. He describes the experience to James as becoming "the sun, the hot sand, green seaweed anchored to a rock, swaying in the tide" (*LDJ* 153). The final image is particularly revealing in this regard. The seaweed, anchored firmly yet swaying in the tide, replicates the condition of the fetus in amniotic fluid. Whether a death wish or a desire to return to the womb (which come to much the same thing), Edmund's ideal disqualifies him as priest-confessor; he cannot grant absolution since, in terms of his desires, at any rate, he is not a full-fledged member of this community.

A second and perhaps more significant reason concerns the confessions themselves. We have said that each of the confessions is the source of new information, for the characters as well as the audience. For the first time we learn what has caused the vicious cycles of acts 1 through 3; we get a momentary glimpse of the Tyrones' past and can finally comprehend the agonies of this long day. However, these new insights do not remove the problem or even relieve the pain. In the final scene, when Edmund reaches out for Mary, telling her that his consumption has been confirmed, she remonstrates gently but impersonally that he must not touch her since she hopes to become a nun. The Tyrones' confessions have not led to forgiveness and reintegration; the family remains hopelessly shattered, its members isolated from each other as well as from the outside world.

The ritual fails because, although the Tyrones share their lost ideals with one another in this final scene, one which is fraught with religious language and presented as a confession, they do not regard what they have done as requiring absolution. Unlike Jim Tyrone in *A Moon for the Misbegotten,* they are not so much confessing sins as they are revealing lost hopes. This varies somewhat from character to character, as we would expect. When James acknowledges his ambition to be a great Shakespearean actor, a goal which was subverted by the easy success of *Monte Cristo,* he simply wonders aloud, with a tinge of sadness, what it was he wanted to buy that was worth so much. Jamie, who acknowledges his ambivalence toward his younger brother, does confess in the strict sense of that word (hence, the greatest concentration of religious language is seen in his speech). But even more fundamental to our understanding of Jamie is his description of the first time he caught Mary taking morphine, the moment that left his youthful innocence irrevocably shattered. Being cast from the kingdom, like Simon's banished prince, he wants to drag Edmund down with him—thus, his ''poisoning'' of his younger brother. Edmund's transcendental experiences and Mary's tacit confession of her dashed dreams as she trails her wedding dress behind her all bespeak not so much a sense of wrongdoing for which they feel remorse as a sense of regret at lost potential.

Moreover, none of them seems to see these ideals as destructive. James can regret being seduced by fame and fortune, for instance, but he never questions the validity of his ambition itself nor recognizes the demands it has made on his family. Jamie's searching for the warm haven of happiness he left behind leads him only to Fat Violet, yet he never questions the value of the search nor seeks a suitable adult replacement for youthful innocence. Mary cannot see the destructiveness of her desire to be a nun, though this is graphically demonstrated to the audience as she rebuffs Edmund's appeal for affection on these grounds, nor can Edmund acknowledge the death wish inherent in his desire for a mystical union with the cosmos.

Because the characters don't see their lost ideals as potentially destructive, indeed, because they aren't so much seeking absolution as they are sharing their disappointment at the hand life has dealt them, these confessions are not efficacious. They are not even confessions, in the strict sense of the word. Mary cannot "go to confession," for instance, since she is not even in the present at the end of the play. Unlike Jim Tyrone in *A Moon*, for whom the past and present overlap, Mary is completely in the past at this point. The "sin" for which she might feel the need for forgiveness, the relapse into her addiction, is committed in the present, but she has left the present behind; she resides in the past, beyond the reach of this fact. For her, ironically, the *present* is memory, dimly recalled, if at all. As she plays her stiff-fingered Chopin waltz, her rheumatism reminds us of her encroaching age and its incumbent limitations, but Mary appears oblivious to this fact. When Edmund grabs her and cries that he has consumption, not a summer cold, we're told that "for a second he seems to have broken through to her. She trembles and her expression becomes terrified" (*LDJ* 174). But then she calls out, "No!" and instantly "she is far away again." At this point, when she makes her comment about hoping to be a nun, we receive the full impact of the destructiveness of of her retreat. THis is not the ritual return which regenerates, but its exact opposite: a return that destroys.

Thus the Tyrones remain trapped in time, and the spiral continues downward. As the play ends, Mary is hopelessly beyond the reach of the three men who love her. The family, though physically united around the table, is tragically shattered. Their sacramental wine is a bottle of whiskey that fails to get them drunk; though they are together, there is no real communion.

This hopeless conclusion is foreshadowed metaphorically in Edmund's long, poetic prelude to his confession. Their card game interrupted by the sounds of Mary roaming the upstairs room, he says to James:

> Yes, she moves above and beyond us, a ghost haunting the past and here we sit pretending to forget, but straining our ears listening for the slightest sound, hearing the fog drip from the eaves like the uneven tick of a rundown, crazy clock—or like the dreary tears of a trollop, spattering in a puddle of stale beer on a honky-tonk table top! (*LDJ* 152)

His language is revealing. Both similies contain water images: the fog and the "dreary tears of a trollop." Throughout the play, fog has been a symbol of isolation, as it is in the speech immediately following where Edmund speaks of being "alone, lost in the fog . . . stumbl[ing] on toward nowhere." Here the dripping of the fog is equated with the "uneven tick of a rundown, crazy clock." Although the clock is "uneven" and "rundown," time still runs its course, even within the isolation that the fog provides. The reason is revealed in the next simile, where the dripping of the fog becomes the "dreary tears of a trollop, spattering in a puddle of stale beer." The trollop suggests Mary, the mother-whore,[18] whose footsteps upstairs have occasioned the speech. The juxtaposition of the trollop, the fog, and the clock explains the Tyrones' desperate need to escape the present.

The effects of Mary's addiction and the family's implicit guilt are intensified by the passing of time (the clock) and lead to individual isolation and alienation (the fog).

Edmund has been able to escape in his transcendent experiences by the sea. The isolation suggested by the fog and the trollop's tears contrast with the feeling of belonging that he experiences while at sea (a third water image). "I belonged, without past or future, within peace and unity and a wild joy," he says. He is able, momentarily, to transcend time.

This, however, does not provide a permanent solution. It is no coincidence that the connotations of other water images in the play are destructive, associated with drinking and the use of drugs. The male Tyrones, for instance, use whiskey to "drown their sorrows." Unfortunately, it doesn't work. Jamie complains that he's "had enough to sink a ship, but can't sink" (*LDJ* 156). When Mary enters the living room in the final scene in her morphine fog, Tyrone says, "I've never known her to drown herself in it as deep as this" (*LDJ* 174). Whether the protective isolation of the fog, the forgetfulness of alcohol or drugs, or the mystical merging with the sea, the alternatives associated with water images are not viable ones.

So the confessions do not prove efficacious, in the last analysis. O'Neill, unflinchingly honest, refuses to force a resolution that does not emanate from the action itself; he will not impose a theophany upon the drama that the play itself does not suggest. Following his vision unflinchingly to its conclusion, O'Neill leaves the Tyrones in darkness. The bitter cycles will continue as before; the future holds no hope. Early in the play Mary says, "The past is the present . . . it's the future, too. We all try to lie out of that but life won't let us" (*LDJ* 87). O'Neill's final tableau of the four haunted Tyrones is one of despair, a long journey into night.

7

A Moon for the Misbegotten:
Journey into Light

In *Eugene O'Neill's New Language of Kinship,* Michael Manheim refers to the autumnal mood of *A Moon for the Misbegotten.* While *Iceman* and *Long Day's Journey,* set in July and August, respectively, are "full of anguish and the torrid heat of summer," he writes, *A Moon for the Misbegotten,* set in September, displays a Keatsian "mellow fruitfulness."[1] The tone is indeed one of quiet acceptance, even affirmation. While *Long Day's Journey* traces the fate of the Tyrones to its desperate conclusion, leaving the family shattered in the final scene, *A Moon,* its sequel, deals with the family history eleven years later, after both James and Mary have died. At this point Edmund has a family of his own, leaving Jamie, the misbegotten son, searching for the peace and acceptance that eluded him within his own family. In dramatizing the final days of his elder brother, the playwright bestows a benediction upon a man he both loved and hated.

O'Neill began writing *A Moon,* the last play he would complete, late in 1941, almost twenty years after his brother's death in 1923. Its composition, like that of its predecessor, was an excruciatingly painful experience; reliving his past, he would often weep over scenes as he wrote. Yet from this agony emerges a drama of deep peace and serenity. As Jamie receives the absolution he so desperately longs for, so, we sense, does the playwright.

Linear Time: The Past as Nemesis

It is interesting, given the serenity of this final play, that it contains many of the elements that contributed to the devastating conflicts of *Long Day's Journey.* In *A Moon,* for instance, Jim Tyrone, like the four Tyrones of the earlier play, locates an ideal in a golden age which is forever lost to him. Jamie, now significantly just "Tyrone," is rapidly drinking himself into an early grave, mourning the loss of his mother and torturing himself over his behavior at the time of her death. After his father died, Tyrone had given up liquor entirely in order to take care of Mary. He had been abstemious for nearly two years when she was taken ill. Overcome by grief, he once again began to drink, a fact of which Mary was aware. ''I know damned well just before she died she recognized me,'' Jamie says. ''She saw I was drunk. Then she closed her eyes so she couldn't see, and was glad to die!''[2] Tyrone reports that he stayed drunk on the long train ride East with his mother's coffin, accompanied on the way by a prostitute whom he refers to bitterly as a ''blonde pig who looked more like a whore than twenty-five whores''; when he arrived he was too drunk to attend Mary's funeral.

The episode with the ''blonde pig'' haunts him, as does the memory of his mother's disgust; he longs for the days before his fall, a period he recalls in idyllic terms. Here, as in *Long Day's Journey,* time betrays Jim, removing him ever further from the only happiness he has ever known.

Josie Hogan, the outsized daughter of a tenant farmer on Tyrone's property, is also at a crisis point in her life. In the play's first scene Josie is at the end of an era and needs to begin again. Twenty-year-old Mike, Josie's youngest brother and the last of three to leave home, is about to sneak off the farm with Josie's help and a handful of cash she has stolen from the ''Old Man.'' Josie has cared for Mike since their mother died giving him birth, and she now helps him escape their domineering father, Phil, whom she loves if her brothers don't. ''I'm sorry to see you go,'' she says, fighting back the tears, ''but it's the best thing for you. That's why I'm helping you, the same as I helped Thomas and John. You can't stand up to the Old Man any more than Thomas or John could, and the old divil would always keep you a slave'' (*Moon* 4).[3] As he leaves, casting off for the big city, his parting injunction is that Josie should settle down, get married, and raise a family of her own.

Mike's leaving clears the way for just that. Josie, twenty-eight years old, in typical Irish fashion became the matriarch when her own mother died. Having raised her three brothers, she is left alone with her father at a time of life when she should be starting a family of her own. On one level, the dramatic action revolves around that very point: Mike's parting jibe about tricking Jim into a shotgun wedding and Phil's comments in a similar vein set up the intrigue of the play. Will Josie and Jim get married, in spite of all the obstacles in their path? It's quickly obvious that they love each other and that if they are to have a lasting relationship, it must be now or never. For Josie as for Jim, the time is ripe.

Although both characters long for the acceptance and love traditionally associated with family, neither has been able to achieve or sustain it. In a sense, both are misbegotten.[4] Josie's problem is physical, at least initially. So large for a woman that she is described in the stage directions as ''almost a freak,'' she is five feet eleven and weighs around one hundred and eighty pounds. She is ''more powerful than any but an exceptionally strong man'' (*Moon* 1). Acutely conscious of her bulk, she makes jokes at her own expense and hides behind a pose of promiscuity and worldly experience. Evidently her rough talk has been convincing, since even Mike believes it, and as none of the suitors whom she has spurned will admit to their rejection, her reputation as a loose woman goes unchallenged. Hiding behind her bold manner, Josie longs for someone who will love her as she is. She is afraid to confess her virginity to Jim, lest he think her too innocent and lose interest.

Jim's problems run much deeper. For him, family has always meant Mary, the mother from whom he was never able to separate. We saw in *Long Day's Journey* that when he learned that she was addicted to morphine, his whole world went sour. He was never to recover the innocence he lost at that critical juncture nor find a suitable adult replacement. Intensely jealous of his father and his younger brother, both of whom demanded and received Mary's love and attention, he sought solace in drink and frequented the whorehouses, but neither satisfied his deep longing for love. When James died and Edmund, now cured of consumption, married and established a life of his own, Jim at last had Mary to himself. For two years, "she had only me to attend to things for her and take care of her," he tells Josie. He even went on the wagon: "She'd always hated my drinking. So I quit. It made me happy to do it. For her. Because she was all I had, all I cared about. Because I loved her" (*Moon* 95).[5] Thus when she dies he not only has to deal with his sense of loss and anger at being abandoned; he must also contend with the intense guilt and self-hatred he feels for having betrayed Mary's faith in him. The misbegotten son, having briefly tasted happiness, can no longer live without it. Like Simon Harford, he is a prince banished from his kingdom; standing outside the door, he can neither enter nor leave.

But Jim is misbegotten in still another sense, one that goes beyond his need for a biological family. Cut off from Mary, James, and Edmund, he is also alienated from his cultural roots. This dimension of Jim's dilemma is focused effectively at his entrance when he exchanges insults with Phil Hogan in a verbal game they clearly both enjoy. The stage direction tells us that Jim's smile has "the ghost of a former youthful, irresponsible Irish charm." His opening line is Latin, a quotation from Virgil's First Eclogue: "Fortunate senex, ergo tua rura manebunt, et tibi magna satis, quamvis lapis omnia nudus" (*Moon* 25). When he translates, he imitates Hogan's brogue. Phil replies, "It's easy to see you've a fine college education. It must be a big help to you, conversing with whores and barkeeps" (*Moon* 25).

These few lines present in condensed form the problem that plagues Tyrone throughout the play. Culturally misbegotten, he feels a part of neither the Celtic nor the American world. Although he has a beguiling Irish smile and the characteristic fondness for rhetorical games, he has to *imitate* Hogan's brogue. His classical education and fine clothes elevate him above Hogan's immigrant status, but here, too, he is schizophrenic. He is a Broadway gambler trying to pass for a Wall Street professional; his college education is incompatible with his whore-and-barkeep friends. Later in the play he will side with Josie and Phil against their neighbor, Harder, a Standard Oil magnate who treats Hogan like a peasant. Yet Jim himself becomes the enemy when Josie thinks he has agreed to sell their farm to the millionaire. Though attracted to the Hogans' Irish ways, for much of the play, Tyrone cannot acknowledge his own ethnic ties.[6]

Jim's cultural ambivalence, a trait which we first observed in *Long Day's Journey* (where he is not only ambivalent, but adamantly anti-Irish), is reinforced by contrast with the Irishness of Josie and Phil. Their language, always Irish in syntax and cadence, is also salted with Gaelic expressions. Phil's love of liquor and Josie's determined but tolerant abstinence represent two halves of the same coin; both are standard Irish responses to drinking. Their love of family and intense loyalty to "old Ireland" are also typical. Josie has "the map of Ireland . . . stamped on her face" (*Moon* 1). Both father and daughter are thoroughly Irish and clearly proud of it.

This is dramatized in a memorable encounter early in the play where, as noted above, O'Neill enacts for us the anecdote Edmund only reports in *Long Day's Journey* (in which it also galvanized, however briefly, the Irish Tyrones against the outsider). Harder, who inherited his fortune and now lives the life of a country gentleman, represents the closest America has come to an aristocracy. As such, the Irish Hogans associate him with the hated English ruling class. When Harder visits them, he is dressed in an English tweed coat and riding boots and carries a riding crop in his hand. He looks for all the world like an overseer visiting a tenant and expects the deference and respect the rich feel is their just due from the poor.

In terms of financial and political power, the T. Stedman Harders of this community clearly have the upper hand. The Hogans' ramshackle farmhouse dramatizes their lowly status. An ugly, splotched, "clapboarded affair," it has been moved to its present site and looks it. It is propped about two feet above ground on timber blocks and is missing panes from every window. Like their house, the Hogans too have been transplanted; they do not belong here.

Yet in a face-to-face confrontation with this spunky pair, Harder hasn't a chance. The scene is a tour-de-force of heavy-handed Irish humor and rhetorical play. Harder has come to complain about Hogan's pigs drinking from his pond, but he barely has a chance to open his mouth. After some introductory name-calling ("Where's your manners, you spindle-shanked jockey?") and ridicule ("I don't think he's a jockey. It's only the funny pants he's wearing"), Josie and Phil employ an old Irish tactic—the solemn, straight-faced treatment of an absurdity. When Harder says, "Listen to me Hogan. I didn't come here—" about to add "to listen to your damned jokes," Hogan interrupts, "What? What's that you said?" (He stares at the dumbfounded Harder with droll amazement, as if he couldn't believe his ears.) "You didn't come here?" (He takes off his hat and scratches his head in comic bewilderment.) "Well, that's a puzzle surely. How d'you suppose he got here?" (*Moon* 38). They finally shove Harder off their land, accusing him of trespassing and "enticing" their pigs to drink his water. McCabe, Harder's Irish groom who watches from the road, "can hardly stay in the saddle for laughing!" (*Moon* 42).

Jim, too, enjoys the sight, but from the safety of Josie's bedroom, where he has retreated, at her suggestion, to avoid antagonizing Harder. Culturally, Tyrone straddles both worlds. Thus the action of the play traces Jim's path back, not just to his mother, but also to the motherland.

Memory and Ritual

When Josie sees Jim approaching their farmhouse from afar, her face softens, the stage directions indicate, and she says, "Look at him when he thinks no one is watching, with his eyes on the ground. Like a dead man walking slow behind his own coffin" (*Moon* 23). It is a key line. In a very real sense, Tyrone is dead from the outset. He is so obsessed with the past that he has given up hope for the future. The relationship between linear time and memory thus functions differently here than in the other cycle plays we have considered. In all of them, the past is determinative in some fashion. Con Melody, Simon Harford, Erie Smith, the bums at Harry Hope's saloon, the Tyrones (with the significant exception of Edmund)—all locate an ideal at a specific moment in the past. Though the nature and the validity of the ideals differ in each case, these characters share the conviction that whatever happiness they have known and perhaps can ever know resides in the past and thus eludes them. They respond differently to this belief, but all in some fashion try to relive the past, either by returning to it or by bringing it into the present.

With Jim, the case is different. As Jamie in *Long Day's Journey*, he confesses his lost innocence and his dream that, if Mary licked her addiction, he might also conquer his. Although not much hope is held out for this possibility, there is still a telling wistfulness about the confession. As Jim Tyrone, all hope is gone. Mary is dead; he cannot have her back, nor can he change what he did before and after her death. A refrain from a sentimental tune from the 1890s keeps running through his head:

> And baby's cries can't waken her
> In the baggage coach ahead. (*Moon* 72)

As he brings Mary's body back East in the long train ride from California, he cannot escape the finality of that fact. Time, for Mary, has run out; the hourglass is empty. And because he is so identified with her, in a real sense Jim dies at the same time.

Thus, for Jim, the past does not hold a promise of wholeness to take the edge off the emptiness of the present moment as it does for the other characters in the cycle. The only golden age Jim can look back to, that brief period of happiness before Mary died, serves merely to mock his present pain. Con Melody can pretend he is "among them but not of them," the boarders can trade pipe dreams about tomorrow, Smith can re-create his relationship with the dead Hughie in the person of Charlie Hughes. Despite the ultimate futility of these measures, they provide momentary solace.

Not for Jim. Since his life ended with Mary's death, the past is rather a source of punishment. The past pursues Tyrone like the Erinyes pursued Orestes; it is his nemesis. He is so obsessed with the memory of the long train ride and the blonde prostitute that the past really is the present for him. His memories are bleak and he looks desperately for relief from the pain they bring.

As the play reaches its climax, this desperation deepens. Jim is two hours late for a moonlight visit he promised Josie, and as she waits, forlorn and humiliated, Phil returns from the local watering hole with the tale that Jim has promised to sell their farm to Harder. At first incredulous, Josie vows to get revenge on Jim by seducing him and tricking him into the shotgun wedding Mike had suggested that morning, with the scheming Phil's encouragement.

When Tyrone does arrive at last, fighting a case of the "heebie-jeebies," as he calls them, there is much talk about this evening being different from all the others each has known. But Jim is haunted by his memories and is having trouble shaking them. "What's come over you, Jim?" Josie asks. "You look as if you've seen a ghost." As he looks away he replies dryly, "I have. My own" (*Moon* 73). He vows to "let the dead past bury its dead" and be present to this evening, but it is not all that easy. Several times, as he talks to Josie, he confuses her with the blonde whore. He cannot differentiate between the past and the present, between memory and time. As he says at one point, "There is no present or future—only the past happening over and over again—now. You can't get away from it" (*Moon* 82–83).

Jim's words echo Nietzsche's doctrine of eternal recurrence, but ironically, in that, while Zarathustra sees the eternal oneness of all moments as a victory over time's tyranny, for Tyrone it is the past which triumphs. His experience of eternal recurrence is one of unending punishment.

This cyclic return is, for Jim, a continuing round of drunken one-night stands. Although Josie is jealous of his pretty "Broadway tarts," as she calls them, they clearly exist only as an indistinguishable sea of faces for Jim. When Josie argues, for instance, that this night could be different for them because of their love for one another, Tyrone demurs that he would poison it for her like he's poisoned all the other nights. "I've seen too God-damned many dawns creeping grayly over too many dirty windows," he says; "slept with drunken tramps on too many nights!" (*Moon* 81 and 78). Even when Josie wakes Jim after their miraculous night together, still half asleep and "dimly conscious of a woman's body" he mutters, "Again, eh? Same old stuff. Who the hell are you, sweetheart?" When

Josie says, "It's dawn," he quotes Dowson's "Cynara" (reminding us of *Long Day's Journey*):

> "But I was desolate and sick of an old passion,
> When I awoke and found the dawn was gray." (*Moon* 107)

He adds with a sneer, "They're all gray. Go to sleep, Kid—and let me sleep."

The one-night stands have not worked. Jim can no more lose himself in a bottle of booze than on a South Sea island, as he himself tells Josie; his memories will always find him. What he seeks is a cycle of a different sort, a return to his origins, both cultural and individual, akin to those that undergird tribal or religious rituals: a return that allows him to step outside both the present moment and memory—or, to be more precise, to transcend time by being simultaneously inside and outside of its boundaries.

His involvement with Josie makes clear that Tyrone senses this need on some level, just as he knows that Josie is the only one who can save him. Because his longings are shaped by cultural as well as personal experience, only an Irish matriarch can grant Jim the absolution that will allow him to come to terms with his past. Thus the play insists on Josie's thoroughly Celtic maternalism. She is depicted as the *magna mater,* even to the detail of physical size, mothering her brothers and assuming the role of "wife" and helpmeet for Phil as well. Her toleration of his drunken antics recalls the patient strength and shrewd wisdom of a Juno Boyle or a Pegeen Mike.

Jim's attitude toward Josie is also typically Irish. His confusion of mother and whore in her person, for instance, reflects the sexual ambivalence often felt by the Irish son toward his mother—an ambivalence also present in *Long Day's Journey.*[7] This is further focused by an allusion Tyrone makes in the midst of his moonlight confession, when he mutters to himself, "Christ, in a minute you'll start singing 'Mother Macree'!" (*Moon* 96).[8] Both Jim's need for Josie and his ambivalence towards her come out of his Irish background.

Thus, when Tyrone comes to Josie for absolution, he is seeking forgiveness from his mother. This accounts for his irritation at Josie's promiscuous pose; as his mother, she must be pure and above reproach. At first Josie does not understand this. When, upon learning that Jim had not betrayed them to Harder, she wants to consummate their love, "a strange change . . . comes over his face. He looks at her now with a sneering cynical lust" (*Moon* 88). Since Tyrone equates sex with lust, he reverts to his Broadway manner: "Sure thing, Kiddo. What the hell else do you suppose I came for? I've been kidding myself. . . . You're the goods, Kid. I've wanted you all along. Love, nuts! I'll show you what love is. I know what you want, Bright Eyes. . . . Come on, Baby Doll, let's hit the hay" (*Moon* 89). When Josie cries out in protest, Tyrone backs off, muttering, "I *was* seeing things. . . . For a moment I thought you were that blonde pig—"

(*Moon* 89). He is only able to accept her love when it is offered on maternal terms; when, in short, Josie becomes Mary, the Irish mother. Understanding at last, Josie says,

> Sure, I was only trying to give you happiness, because I love you. I'm sorry I was so stupid and didn't see—But I see now, and you'll find I have all the love you need. [*She gives him a hug and kisses him. There is passion in her kiss but it is a tender, protective maternal passion, which, he responds to with an instant grateful yielding.*]
> Tyrone [*Simply*]: Thanks, Josie. You're beautiful. I love you. I knew you'd understand. (*Moon* 91)

Josie, in turn, can only accept Jim when she knows that he's "Irish," i.e., when she learns that he has not betrayed her to the landlord. Tyrone becomes a legitimate lover, and she wants to give herself to him in the moonlight. But this is the chaste moon of Diana; their love, which is to know no consummation, cannot produce children. In this climactic scene, since Josie functions as virgin-mother and lover, Mary as well as herself, physical consummation is impossible. Their union and the generation of their family occur instead when Tyrone confesses his sins.

At this point, as in *Long Day's Journey*, O'Neill employs the rite of confession to shape the scene and chooses language with religious overtones. In this play, however, the pattern of confession and absolution moves toward a cosmogony, the creation of a new order.

As Tyrone leans back, his head on Josie's breast, his confession pours forth at last. It is punctuated with "religious" expletives: "For God's sake—" (*Moon* 98); "Christ" (*Moon* 94 and 96). Josie in turn says, "For the love of God—" (*Moon* 98), as the whole sordid story comes out at last: the "blonde pig" and his failure to attend the funeral. At length Tyrone implores, "She'd understand and forgive me, don't you think? She always did. She was simple and kind and pure of heart. She was beautiful. You're like her deep in your heart. That's why I told you" (*Moon* 98–99).

It is almost as hard a confession to hear as to make, and at first Josie is repulsed. Finally, however, she understands and so fulfills her role as mother-confessor. She now "bends over him with a brooding maternal tenderness" and "speaks soothingly as she would to a child . . . in a tender, crooning tone like a lullaby." Tyrone's face is "calm with the drained exhausted peace of death" (*Moon* 100), and the first phase of confession is complete. He lays his burden of guilt at Josie's feet, reconciled with his family at last.[9]

Act 4 presents an absolution and renewal, the second phase of the rite of confession. This is to be a sunrise unlike the grey dawns of Dowson's "Cynara." Instead, Josie, the virgin-mother/lover, cradles Tyrone in her arms Madonna-like. "The two make a strangely tragic picture in the wan dawn light—this big sorrowful woman hugging a haggard-faced, middle-aged drunkard against her breast, as if he were a sick child'' (*Moon* 101). She has now assumed the identity of another Mary—the Blessed Virgin. Later she explains this miracle to Hogan: ''A virgin who bears a child in the night, and the dawn finds her still a virgin. If that isn't a miracle, what is?'' (*Moon* 103). Josie's statement emphasizes the mythic quality of this experience—a moment simultaneously in and out of time. She is Mary Tyrone and the Virgin Mary; the ''virgin mother'' who was lost is found.

It is the confessional ritual that allows for this transformation of Josie. In the sacrament, past, present and future exist simultaneously. As the penitent is reconciled to God, he ''dies to sin'' and is born again. The ritual action, because it establishes by its premises an *illud tempus,* vanquishes the power of Chronos and leads to a cosmogony. Thus a death-resurrection archetype underlies the climax of *A Moon for the Misbegotten.* As Tyrone himself explains to Josie, he is already dead when he arrives at the Hogans; his drinking is an effort to hasten the physical extinction he has already embraced psychologically. But the death he experiences in the moonlight, cast in the confessional framework, is of a different sort. He lays his sins to rest, and with a free conscience at last, sleeps the dreamless sleep of a newborn child, awakening reborn, with a new sense of peace and harmony.[10]

At first he denies the validity of his resurrection. Only half awake, as we noted earlier, he quotes Dowson and mutters without opening his eyes, ''Again, eh? Same old stuff'' (*Moon* 107). Fully conscious, however, he tries to understand what has transpired: ''It's hard to describe how I feel. It's a new one on me. Sort of at peace with myself and this lousy life—as if all my sins had been forgiven—'' (*Moon* 110). His cynicism reasserts itself briefly, and he quips sarcastically as he looks at the glowing sunrise, ''God seems to be putting on quite a display. I like Belasco better. Rise of curtain, Act-Four stuff'' (*Moon* 111). Even this self-conscious line, however, recalls the conclusion of David Belasco's production of *The Passion,* in which James O'Neill reenacted the crucifixion of Christ. ''Rise of curtain, Act Four'' of *A Moon for the Misbegotten* presents another resurrection story.[11] When Jim does recall his confession in the moonlight, he is at first beset with shame and anguish. But finall; able to accept Josie's love, he asks for forgiveness one more time and testifies to the change the night has wrought: ''Forgive me, Josie. I do remember! I'm glad I remember! I'll never forget your love! . . . Never! . . . Never, do you hear! I'll always love you, Josie. . . . Goodbye—and God bless you!'' (*Moon* 113).

His last words to Josie are a benediction, as are hers to him. As she watches him disappear down the road, she says gently, ''May you have your wish and die in your sleep soon, Jim, darling. May you rest forever in forgiveness and peace'' (*Moon* 115).[12] Thus *A Moon* ends as it begins, but with a significant difference. Mike, who leaves at the play's beginning, is only Josie's son by proxy; she serves as a mother substitute until he is old enough to sever the umbilical cord and set out to seek his fortune. By the play's end, Josie has given birth to a son of her own, for, though there is no blood tie with Jim, she has given him new life. He leaves Josie as he must, but he takes with him the peace and forgiveness he has found in her arms. Mike's admonition that Josie should have a family of her own has, ironically, come to pass. As Tyrone accepts both his cultural and personal heritage in his union with Josie, they come together to form a family in which opposites are reconciled and ideals are within reach. Josie can simultaneously be virgin, mother, and lover; Jim can be child and adult, son and suitor.

The resurrection, however, is not just Jim Tyrone's. As a composite figure representing James, Jamie, and Edmund Tyrone/O'Neill,[13] his reintegration into the community includes the entire family. In bringing peace to Tyrone, O'Neill stills the ghosts of "all the four haunted Tyrones" and, by extension, all the O'Neills as well. Thus in *A Moon for the Misbegotten* he resolves the stalemate that concludes *Long Day's Journey into Night.*

Although both plays use the Catholic ritual of confession, the confession in *Long Day's Journey* fails, while in *A Moon* it proves successful. The difference lies partially in the cultural attitudes embodied in each play. The Jamie of *Long Day's Journey* is never able to accept his Irish heritage. As long as his father is alive, Jamie maligns the "old country" to antagonize him. His rebellion against James and Ireland manifests a single attitude; as both son and second generation immigrant he must sever connections with his past to establish his own identity. Jim Tyrone of *A Moon,* though he is culturally ambivalent during much of the play, ultimately embraces both his cultural and familial heritage in his confession to Josie. In *A Moon for the Misbegotten,* O'Neill has fully returned to his own cultural roots for the framework of the action. Not only is the conclusion of the play structured by the Catholic confessional ritual; Tyrone's experience of the ritual is Irish, as well. The American reliance on rationality in *Long Day's Journey,* the assumption that to reveal the origins of the pain will eradicate the pain itself, is replaced by an Irish relinquishment to the arational, the mysterious. The confession becomes what it should be, what it is in its Irish context: an act of faith. Jim intuits that Josie can save him. She is Irish mother, and he finally acknowledges his need of her. Thus Tyrone can become a son of Ireland as well as of his biographical family. As such, the entire family receives absolution. Josie can be Mary Tyrone and the Virgin Mary simultaneously, for instance, an ideal impossible for the Mary of *Long Day's Journey,* because she has the proper Irish attitude. Josie wants a family and thus, though virgin, is blessed with a son, while Mary Tyrone's attraction to the Virgin represents an escape from her role as *magna mater.*

Moreover, Jim's confession also involves an act of contrition. The Tyrones of *Long Day's Journey,* as we have seen, do not so much confess sins for which they feel the need of absolution as they reveal lost ideals and shattered dreams. Further, they are unable to see the destructiveness of these ideals. Tyrone, on the other hand, is excruciatingly aware of the effect that his relapse into drunkenness had on Mary before she died and experiences intense guilt about the "blonde pig" incident, which he regards as a betrayal of his mother. He cannot change the outcome of the events that surrounded her death and its aftermath, but he needs to make peace with himself about the part that he played. He needs, in short, forgiveness, which is what confession offers. Because Jim comes to Josie with an awareness of his need for absolution and because she, unlike Edmund, is an appropriate confessor, the ritual produces its mysterious effect.

Thus O'Neill's dramas reveal that, within an Irish context, the Tyrones (i.e., O'Neills) have the necessary cultural supports to cope with life's adversities. Unfortunately, like Phil Hogan's small "praties,"[14] their cultural transplantation results in a diminishment. It is only in his plays that the dramatist can resolve the tragedy of his long-dead family, but this, at least, is granted him. As his last drama ends, the sky is "glowing with all the colors of an exceptionally beautiful sunrise" (*Moon* 111); the fog-shrouded midnight of *Long Day's Journey* ends in the radiant dawn of *A Moon for the Misbegotten*.

8

Possessors Dispossessed:
The Banished Prince

The characters in O'Neill's final dramas, like the playwright himself, seek the grail of peace and wholeness, longing for an ideal which seems always just out of reach. Like Miniver Cheevy, they "sigh for what is not," but unlike Robinson's would-be knight their problem is not that they are born too late. Their dilemma and that of the culture at large, as O'Neill portrays it, stems from being in time and longing for an ideal which is not.

The image that best conveys this yearning for the ideal, for the moment of innocence regained, is that of the prince banished from his kingdom in Deborah Harford's fairy tale. The lost kingdom represents an Edenic paradise of harmony and peace; fertility and plenty; love, acceptance, and belonging. It is Jung's "green world." Its opposite, what the young prince fears he will find behind the magic door, is a wasteland of perpetual night, a barren desert echoing with the derisive laughter of the witch.

The prince, as noted earlier, recalls the archetypal romantic hero, questing for the grail. He is Adam, desiring to reenter the garden; he is Cain, the exile and outcast; Christ, the second Adam; Everyman, seeking the kingdom of heaven. He is also the American Adam, searching for the Promised Land of realized hopes and dreams come true. His fate rests upon his ability to distinguish truth from falsehood. Is the enchantress lying? Is the image of former bliss an illusion that will disintegrate into dust once the door is opened, the mystery solved? That it is a woman who holds the key is significant. Whether beautiful enchantress or wicked witch (a decision O'Neill refuses to make: Deborah's final motives for entering the summer-house, whether altruistic or selfish, are left ambiguous), a matriarch presides over this heavenly kingdom, a realm which once belonged to the young king.

The sources of this fairy tale are two-fold. Biographically, its blissful innocence is based in O'Neill's own childhood experience. Being sent away to boarding school at age seven and discovering his mother's addiction at fifteen were, according to the playwright, pivotal experiences which thrust him into the harsh

world of reality. O'Neill's personal longing for lost innocence is reflected in Simon
Harford's desire to enter the summer-house with Deborah, to return to a womblike
state "beyond separations." The fact that it is a woman who has dispossessed
the young king and now stands between him and his lost realm echoes O'Neill's
own ambivalence toward his mother.

From a cultural perspective, the young prince is an apt analogue to the
American Adam. The scriptural language used by the early Puritan settlers to
refer to America—the New Jerusalem, the New Canaan, the City on the Hill—
reveals their vision of the New World as man's last chance to establish the kingdom
of God on earth. The Old World was corrupt, degenerate; the New World held
out a chance to start over again.

We are the inheritors of these dreams and aspirations, though the centuries
have stripped away the spiritual foundation on which they were based. What remains is a vague emptiness, a longing for a nebulous and ill-defined utopia which
Americans assume as their birthright. This is the country, as the myth would
have it, where anyone can become president, where the rags-to-riches dream can
come true. The Statue of Liberty welcomes the world's tired, poor, and hungry
into New York Harbor and offers them infinite possibility. It is this sense of ex-
pectation and excitement that Fitzgerald captures in Jay Gatsby, whose salient
characteristic is his "heightened sensitivity to the promises of life." His ability
to dream the impossible and expect it to come true is thoroughly American.

The dream, however, as Fitzgerald understood, is greater than any realization of it. It represents an ideal that began to recede into the past even as the
Dutch sailors set foot on the green breast of the New World. The ideal can exist
as ideal only insofar as it is ahistorical. In this regard, unlike the biographical
wellspring of the fairy tale, the cultural component has no corresponding basis
in reality. The young prince once claimed and experienced this kingdom, now
lost; his misery in being dispossessed lies precisely in the fact that his former
glory shimmers tantalizingly before him. What he must do is recapture his past,
reclaim his birthright. Our own beginnings at Jamestown and Plymouth, in Rhode
Island and Salem, however, represent periods of privation, hardship, and suffering. The American dream romanticizes this past and places its hope in the future.
As an ideal, it shapes a set of values, attitudes and expectations that inform the
aspirations of our institutions and customs, our literature and art, our self-image
in public and private; as with all ideals, it is able to reconcile opposites and encompass the whole precisely because it is not subject to limitations of time and
space, but looks toward an infinite horizon.

In his plays O'Neill cannot reconcile himself to the fact that the ideal remains forever out of reach. The biographical and cultural components of his experience intersect in the fairy tale of the dispossessed prince and illustrate his
ambivalence. From the biographical perspective, the lost kingdom, once known,
can be regained by a return to the past; from the cultural, it cannot, since the

kingdom lies in the future. Hence the ambiguity surrounding the enchantress and her threat: the dream may or may not turn out to be an illusion; the paradise lost may be, when recovered, barren wasteland, because what was may not determine what will be. All dreams thus become suspect—necessary for comfort and survival, perhaps, but ultimately empty lies. Because the individual, unlike the culture, has a limited future, the dreams of Harry Hope and his cronies, the self-delusion of Smith and Hughes, the Byronic posing of Con Melody, and the poetry of Deborah and Simon Harford are bounded by death and darkness in the end. The curse is that they cannot live without at least the memory of the kingdom. The hope that the past can be recovered in the future, and the fear that it cannot, keeps them forever beggars standing outside the door, afraid to enter and unable to leave.

The biographical and the cultural aspects of the fairy tale mark the path that O'Neill traveled in the final decade of his career. His last two major bursts of creative energy involved the historical cycle, an articulation of his version of American history, and a cluster of plays dealing with his own life experience. That these two enterprises are related in theme and intent comes as no surprise, though O'Neill himself apparently was not aware of a connection at the outset. On June 5, 1939, after almost five continuous years of work on the historical cycle, he put it aside to work on a play that had "nothing to do with" it; the next day he noted in his *Work Diary* his intention of doing outlines of two new dramas which were to become *The Iceman Cometh* and *Long Day's Journey into Night*. At some point O'Neill may have become aware of the interconnectedness of the two enterprises; Bogard, for instance, points out that O'Neill talked of assembling a repertoire company for the whole cycle, engaging actors and actresses for several seasons to mount and produce the entire work. Even just on the basis of physical type, he writes, "it can be suggested that O'Neill thought of the company as playing not only the cycle, but the autobiographical plays as well, including *Hughie* and *The Iceman Cometh*."[1] The strong physical resemblances of Deborah Harford and Mary Tyrone, Cornelius Melody and James Tyrone, Sr., Simon Harford and Edmund Tyrone, Sara Melody and Josie Hogan, and Erie Smith and Theodore Hickman does indeed suggest that the dramatist intended the historical and the autobiographical plays to be produced as a single unit.

That the plays deal with similar concerns, raise many of the same questions, and show marked similarities in character types and relationships is clear.[2] What remains to be seen is the precise manner in which these cycles intersect.

In terms of their composition, it is significant that O'Neill begins with the history plays, whose emphasis is primarily on the repetitive aspects of human experience. Though of course each drama focuses on the linear experience of individuals, the movement of *Possessors* as a whole is cyclic. At the same time, any cultural history embodies a paradox: The experience of the culture can be seen as fundamentally cyclic; events (wars, uprisings, revolutions) as well as social, political, economic, and ideological movements repeat themselves, with variations, *ad infinitum.* Yet while this perspective focuses on the cyclic nature of cultural experience, it is equally true that, for the culture at large, history goes on forever; there is no endpoint. Thus time carries the culture forward on the linear continuum while it simultaneously repeats the patterns of the past.

O'Neill explores this paradox in the lives of his cycle characters, Con Melody and Simon and Ethan Harford, trying to come to grips with the crucial questions this raises: How free is the individual to shape his/her own destiny in the face of historical forces (generally "his," since all of O'Neill's cycle protagonists are male)? What happens if his cultural history pulls him forward (Jonathan and the steamboat) while his familial history pulls him back (Ethan's touch-of-the-poet allegiance to the clippership)?

As he worked through the historical plays, O'Neill's focus was on the individual-in-community, fleshing out his view of America's self-destructive seeking after material wealth and power from generation to generation. As the years passed, however, the cycle kept getting larger. It knew no boundaries, and, expanding ever forward and backward in time, it would not come right. There was no end to this history, no final word.

At length, in desperation O'Neill turned to two much smaller communities (smaller, that is, on a literal level, though universal in their implications): a dozen-odd societal dropouts on the West Side of New York; a family of four in a summer vacation cottage. At this point, he draws upon personal memories rather than cultural ones, turning to and creating a history of a different sort than the one that had occupied him for the previous five years. It is, of course, true that the historical plays drew heavily upon his personal past (as in the parallels between Deborah and Mary/Ella, Simon and Edmund/Eugene, and so forth), and the autobiographical plays present an equally valid portrait of the New York-New England subculture, a further indication of the connectedness of these plays.

But as he shifts his focus from a cultural to a more personal history, O'Neill's concerns with the workings of time shift, too. If the context of the earlier plays (earlier, that is, in terms of their conception and initial drafting, not necessarily their completion) is that of the culture at large and the individual within the historical context, his focus narrows to the individual within a smaller unit and a single generation. The individual in both cases must deal with his own mortality, but in the *Possessors* cycle although the individual life ended, the generations continued. With the later plays, *Iceman* and *Hughie, Journey* and *Moon,* the individual stands face to face with the fact that sooner or later, time must stop for *him.* Both deal with linear and cyclic dimensions of experience, with time and memory, but as he works through these issues in an historical context the focus narrows increasingly to the individual experience and the inescapable fact of mortality. It would seem, then, that from a compositional standpoint the historical plays serve as a preparation for the issues O'Neill had been approaching for most—perhaps all—of his career: his own past and his own inevitable death.

Mortality and the Need for Ritual

Given this progression and the need to transcend time as we have traced it throughout these plays, it is interesting to note that the increasing directness with which O'Neill employs autobiographical material is paralleled by his increasingly direct inclusion of ritual. In *A Touch of the Poet* (begun in 1935 and revised up through 1942), Con's incantatory recitation of the "Childe Harold" passage and the anniversary celebration of Talavera function as rituals manqué; though they have sacramental features (the physical props and apotheotic narrative, for instance), they are not fully realized rituals and hence can have no lasting effect. Even less suggestion of ritual occurs in *More Stately Mansions*—whose icon of the Edenic garden suggests the need for forgiveness but provides no vehicle for it—and *The Calms of Capricorn*, whose final scene between Ethan and Sara again demonstrates the emptiness of a world which does not allow for purgation and renewal.

As he moves through these plays to the autobiographical dramas, conceived and written from 1939 to 1943, his use of ritual, specifically the sacrament of confession, becomes increasingly explicit. In *The Iceman Cometh* there are not one, but two confessions; Hickey's recanted and Parritt's not, although both go off to die as the curtain rings down. *Long Day's Journey* concludes with the much-analyzed confession of James, Jamie, and implicitly, Mary, to Edmund, but in this drama, as we have said, the confession confers no redemptive grace. Only in *A Moon for the Misbegotten*, O'Neill's last completed play, is a mythic moment successfully dramatized. The ritual that climaxes in act 3 fuses past, present, and future in a moment of rebirth. Tyrone's individual and cultural histories merge in the present moment, and, as the silver mantle of forgiveness envelopes this "holy family," the potential for renewal incorporates the future as well. This *kairos* effects a redemption of time, delivering Tyrone from the prison of his history. The tragic conclusions of the earlier plays give way to a resurrection in *A Moon for the Misbegotten;* this final drama ends with the rosy dawn of a new day.

That Tyrone achieves peace at last is due to the purgation he experiences in his confession to Josie; his need for a ritual *per se* stems from the failure of both time and memory to save him. In chronological time, as we have noted time and again, the hoped-for Messiah does not arrive, in whatever form. Indeed, because most of the characters in these plays locate a golden age in the past, the future holds forth not hope, but increased distance from "the good." Ethan, the only completely future-oriented character, ends his own life in despair.

In the same way memory, which promises comfort and does provide solace of a sort, actually proves to be an accomplice of the enemy. It is the human faculty that turns linear movement into cyclic movement. This occurs variously. For the Tyrones, memories of the past generate the accusational cycles that shatter any hope for familial unity. Because they live in the past, they cannot forget past ills; because they locate personal ideals (or the loss of one, in Jamie's case) in history, they cannot live in the present or move forward into the future. For Erie Smith and Harry and his friends, living in memory precludes the acceptance of change and flux, the potential of the present moment. For virtually all of the characters (*Calms* excepted), the ultimate result of memory, the lure of the past as it confronts the disappointments of the present, precipitates the return-to-origins that structures these final plays with such consistency: a return to pipe dreams, to a state of childhood innocence, to a former social status, to the womb of the universe, and, finally, a mythic return to a rebirth through a virgin-mother's forgiveness. Although the meaning of the structure varies with each play, the pattern itself is identical as each drama explores a means of transcending the limitations of time. In each instance, the strong chronological movement of the play, narrowing in focus from the nine years of *More Stately Mansions* to the noon-to-dawn period of *A Moon for the Misbegotten,* is countered by the psychological regression of the characters. As the characters attempt to engage their pasts, generally associated with a desire for a merger with a community or with the cosmos at large, their encounter with the past negates the present and turns time back on itself.

Thus the historical and the autobiographical plays present two sides of the same coin: the individual within the historical context, the one and the many, the linear and the cyclic, all of which lead variously but inevitably to the question of mortality, of time's end. The final and most fundamental link in the historical-autobiographical dramas, then, is their shared quest for a means of transcending time and space, an answer to calendar and memory. It is fundamentally a spiritual quest, as these are, at root, plays about the spirit, rather than the psyche, which accounts for the frequency with which O'Neill employs ritual in these dramas. The inclusion of ritual suggests that the only hope of resolving the time-memory impasse lies in the regenerative potential of the mythic experience. This power is available within a ritual context in that it offers a return to origins, an *illud tempus* in which the world is recreated and the individual renewed within the community. A return through memory repeats, but does not restore, the past. Thus, while the structures of all these final plays excepting *Calms* include returns, only *A Moon for the Misbegotten* includes a mythic return to origins.

The critical and final question becomes, then, why does the ritual take hold in *A Moon* while it fails in the other dramas? The answer, as chapter 7 suggests, has to do with Tyrone's return, not just to his family, but to his cultural roots as well. In *A Moon for the Misbegotten,* the two thrusts of the historical-autobiographical endeavor come together in a harmonious relationship: the individual can and finally does find the supports he needs within his cultural situation to confront the past and move forward, purged and unencumbered, into the future. O'Neill at length turns to the culture he left behind and the religion he rejected. Within the context of Irish Catholicism, a milieu hospitable to dreams and mystery, to miracles of the sort Josie describes to Phil—a virgin bearing a dead child in the night and remaining virgin—Jim's rebirth can be accomplished.

The fact that both personal and cultural roots are tapped in this mysterious process is key. Jim is misbegotten culturally as well as individually, as we have said, and needs reconciliation on both counts. But even more to the point, by definition rituals require believing communities; their power flows from the community back to the community again. Neither individuals nor families can generate their own rituals, in the strict sense of this word. Although over the years they may produce traditional patterns of behavior, these behaviors do not operate on the same level as the sacramental rituals of Christianity, for instance, or the fertility rites of prehistorical peoples, whose power derives from the universal consent of the participants. As *Long Day's Journey into Night* so movingly demonstrates, the family cannot successfully generate its own ritual if the appropriate cultural context is not available. Thus here, too, the dual concerns of O'Neill's cycle come together. The individual in need of purgation finds it in the context of community, as we see in *A Moon for the Misbegotten*. By breaking the hold of time and memory, as well as the polarities subsumed in this division, O'Neill's drama achieves a moment of transcendence and regeneration.

After this moment, however, Tyrone leaves, with Josie staring after, bereft and alone, and his departure is tantamount to a final leave-taking from life itself. The peace he has found is genuine; the moonlit moment has been salvific. But its impact is mitigated, in the last analysis, by our awareness of Tyrone's impending death and, even more importantly, of the cultural context of his renewal. Thus, while the means of salvation offered in *A Moon for the Misbegotten* works for Jim Tyrone, it only works in an Irish community. This may account for the rather mild critical reception of *A Moon*, one of O'Neill's finest plays. For while O'Neill speaks eloquently of the need for salvation, of the American Adam seeking readmission to the Garden, his solution ultimately excludes the audience, as, to a lesser extent, it excludes O'Neill himself. The American dream looks to the future; the immigrant resides in the past. The cultural strategies of the Old Country no longer apply to contemporary Americans, even Irish-Catholic Americans. Thus while *A Moon for the Misbegotten* focuses a problem central to the American experience and resolves it in the dramatic action, it ironically requires a return not available to the audience.

It must also be acknowledged, lest O'Neill's progression from the historical dramas up through the integration Tyrone achieves in this final play seem steady and unerring, that he is composing the fairly cynical *Hughie* and continuing to revise *Poet* and *Mansions* up through the early 1940s. The issues he is addressing are too complex and his own stake in them too deep-seated to allow for a single solution to suffice; the psyche—not to mention the creative process—is seldom that tidy.

O'Neill's dramas offer no magic formulae. What they do and do brilliantly is focus the dilemma of the American experience. Drawn onward in hope of the grail and borne back by our ideals into the past, we search our histories, both cultural and individual, seeking peace but desiring possession. Like the prince of the fairy tale, we stand before the door, uncertain whether the kingdom lies in the irrecoverable past or is still to come.

Notes

Chapter 1

1. F. Scott Fitzgerald, *The Great Gatsby* (New York: Charles Scribner's Sons, 1925) 25.

2. Fitzgerald, 182.

3. In her excellent linguistic analysis of his canon, Chothia notes with interest the fact that (with a few minor exceptions) O'Neill only turns to the dialect he knew best, the Irish, in the plays of his maturity. See Jean Chothia, *Forging a Language: A Study of the Plays of Eugene O'Neill* (Cambridge: Cambridge University Press, 1979).

4. Eugene O'Neill, *A Touch of the Poet* (New Haven: Yale University Press, 1955) 99. All subsequent quotations will be taken from this edition and included parenthetically in the text with the designation *Poet.*

5. Eugene O'Neill, *Long Day's Journey into Night* (New Haven: Yale University Press, 1955) 87. All subsequent quotations will be taken from this edition and included parenthetically in the text with the designation *LDJ.*

6. For a detailed history of the composition of the cycle plays and a summary of the time period covered by each, consult Travis Bogard's *Contour in Time: The Plays of Eugene O'Neill* (New York: Oxford University Press, 1972) 371–81; Virginia Floyd's *Eugene O'Neill at Work: Newly Released Ideas for Plays* (New York: Frederick Ungar Publishing Co., 1981) 169–73 and 215–22; *Eugene O'Neill: Work Diary*, vol. 1 (1924–33) and vol. 2 (1934–43), transcribed by Donald Gallup (New Haven: Yale University Library, 1981); and Gallup's introduction to *The Calms of Capricorn* (New Haven and New York: Ticknor and Fields, 1982) vii–xiii. For a summary of the probable content of each play, see Bogard and also John J. Fitzgerald, "The Bitter Harvest of O'Neill's Projected Cycle," *The New England Quarterly*, 40 (September 1967): 364–74.

7. Mircea Eliade, *The Myth of the Eternal Return or, Cosmos and History* (Princeton: Princeton University Press, 1954) 1–34.

8. One critical distinction here: unlike that of O'Neill's characters, the eternal return of premodern people is to a past outside of time, *illud tempus,* not to a point on the linear continuum. This distinction will become key in determining why the return to origins as it is experienced in the context of these plays does not have the regenerative potential of the rituals practiced by Eliade's archaic civilizations.

9. Friedrich Nietzsche, *Thus Spake Zarathustra*, trans. Thomas Common (New York: The Modern Library, n.d.) II "Redemption," section 1.

10. Nietzsche, III, "The Convalescent," section 2.

11. Thomas J. J. Altizer, "Eternal Recurrence and Kingdom of God," David B. Allison, ed., *The New Nietzsche* (Cambridge, Massachusetts: The MIT Press, 1985) 245.

12. It can be argued that Ethan's suicidal plunge into the sea at this play's end represents a symbolic return to the origins of life itself, but as I shall point out in chapter 4, his own rhetoric does not encourage this interpretation.

Chapter 2

1. Harford suggests they move to Ohio, a way-station for streams of Irish immigrants in the mid-nineteenth century—including the families of both Ella Quinlan and James O'Neill.

2. Like Jamie Tyrone in *Long Day's Journey,* another third generation immigrant, sociologically speaking, Sara uses her Irish heritage as a weapon against her father.

3. It is these Yankee traits that link Sara with the last major character of *Poet,* Deborah Harford, and which account for the otherwise inexplicable parallels between the two. We note, for instance, the interesting fact that Sara shares Deborah's admiration of Napoleon, in spite of the fact that Con fought on the British side. Like Deborah, Sara does not take seriously Simon's plan to transform the world with his idealistic dreams. Most importantly, her desire for freedom through power, which she locates in marrying Simon, parallels Deborah's fantasy of wielding control by winning the love of a Napoleon or a Louis XIV. Thus Sara can understand Deborah's motives when the innocent Nora cannot. When Nora protests that Deborah's coming against her husband's orders shows that she is on Simon's side, Sara answers, "Don't be so simple, Mother. Wouldn't she tell Simon that anyway, even if the truth was her husband sent her to do all she could to get him away from me?" (*Poet* 79). She is even capable of adopting Deborah's tactics in the battle for Simon's love: "I've got to be as big a liar as she was. I'll have to pretend I liked her and I'd respect whatever advice she gave him. I mustn't let him see—" (*Poet* 88). As O'Neill works back and forth in his mind from *More Stately Mansions* to *A Touch of the Poet,* he incorporates in the younger Sara those characteristics that would make her capable of the cultural reversal she undergoes in the later play.

4. O'Neill's allusion to this particular poem is apt in more ways than one. Byron, previously society's darling, writes "Childe Harold" from exile, a situation that bears striking parallels to Con's.

5. This is the position drawn upon by T. E. Hulme, for instance, in his famous essay "Classicism and Romanticism" (1924) in which he defines the classical perspective as one emerging from a view of human beings as inherently flawed, bound by limitations, as opposed to the romantic notion of infinite possibility.

6. That O'Neill regarded Con's choice as a diminishment—and permanent—is suggested by the opening scene of his uncut third draft of *More Stately Mansions,* which was included in the play's 1964 Broadway production. Jamie Cregan, mourning Con's premature death only a few short years after the Harford duel, says this at his funeral:

   He could have drunk a keg a day and lived for twenty years yet, if the pride and spirit wasn't killed inside him ever since the night that he tried to challenge that Yankee coward Harford to a duel and him and me got beat by the police and arrested. (Quoted in Michael Manheim, *Eugene O'Neill's New Language of Kinship* [Syracuse: Syracuse University Press, 1982] 116)

7. In Sara's seduction of Simon (which, as we learn in *More Stately Mansions,* results in a pregnancy), Nora's illicit affair with Con is repeated. Sara "becomes" Nora (hence, the similarity of their names and the unusual spelling of "Sara"). It may be an act which has a consecration all its

own, to quote Hester Prynne; certainly Nora—and the audience—understand Sara's willingness to sacrifice everything for love. And it teaches Sara the wisdom of Nora's earlier statement that love was when ''if all the fires of hell was between you, you'd walk in them gladly to be with him and sing with joy at your own burnin', if only his kiss was on your mouth!'' (*Poet* 25). Sara even uses the same rhetoric when she describes her love for Simon. When Nora remonstrates that God will punish her for her sin, Sara replies, ''Let Him! If He'd say to me, for every time you kiss Simon you'll have a thousand years in hell, I wouldn't care, I'd wear out my lips kissing him!'' (*Poet* 149).

But there are also ominous undertones associated with the seduction. We have seen that Con throws their hasty marriage up to Nora and that she is convinced she will suffer in hell for it. This is a fact that bodes ill for Sara. Indeed, we will see in *Mansions* that the parallel holds true: Simon accuses Sara of using her body to force him to marry her—an issue which comes between them.

Chapter 3

1. Eugene O'Neill, *More Stately Mansions* (New Haven: Yale University Press, 1964) 99. This study is based on the Yale University Press edition of *Mansions*, which was shortened for production at the request of Carlotta O'Neill by Karl Ragnar Gierow, then the director of the Swedish Royal Dramatic Theatre, where it received its world première in Stockholm on November 9, 1962. Gierow worked from O'Neill's partly revised third draft of the play; the first typed version. The dramatist burned the first two drafts, both longhand, in February 1943, along with drafts of the first two cycle plays; the typed version, inadvertently included in a box of material sent to the O'Neill collection at Yale, escaped destruction. According to Gallup, the collection curator at that time, Gierow's acting version of the play (in Swedish translation) represents less than half of O'Neill's typed script (which was as long as *Strange Interlude*); much of the omitted material, he adds, was already marked for deletion by O'Neill himself.

    When Mrs. O'Neill agreed that a reading text be made available to students of modern drama, Gallup undertook the task of editing Gierow's acting version and establishing the English equivalent of the Swedish text. See Gallup's introduction to the play (pp. vii–xii) for further details on the publication history as well as the differences between O'Neill's last draft and the Gierow-Gallup text.

    Subsequent citations in the text, abbreviated *MSM,* refer to this edition. See also Louis Sheaffer, *O'Neill: Son and Artist* (Boston: Little, Brown, 1973) 15 and 441.

    An annotated, unexpurgated version of *More Stately Mansions,* edited by Martha Bower, will be published in Fall 1988 by Oxford University Press.

2. Arthur and Barbara Gelb, *O'Neill* (New York: Harper and Brothers, 1962) 801.

3. Commentators disagree about the position of *More Stately Mansions* in O'Neill's canon. Both Jean Chothia and Donald Gallup consider it more typical of the cycle than *A Touch of the Poet,* which O'Neill rewrote in 1942 in order to get at least one cycle play ''definitely and finally finished,'' as he put it in his *Work Diary*; this, after completing *Long Day's Journey* and *Iceman.* Looking at *Mansions* as representative, Chothia locates the cycle in O'Neill's middle period, basing her conclusion partly on the playwright's letter to Robert Sisk, written in July 1935, which associates the cycle with such plays as the *Electra* trilogy and *Great God Brown,* and partly on dramatic qualities of the play. It is, for instance, written in what Chothia calls General American; it covers a long period of time, with characters aging visibly on stage; monologues and asides are employed—all techniques typical of the middle period.

    Michael Manheim regards *Mansions* as a transitional play, with the Sara/Deborah relationship anticipating the rhythm of kinship in evidence in the late plays and Simon's abstract, philosophical approach to life experience as a middle period remnant.

My own position is that while *More Stately Mansions* does retain elements typical of the middle period—notably, the long monologues and asides and the handling of time and on-stage aging—its overall thrust and focus place it more properly in the plays of the late period. O'Neill worked on it over a six-year period, from 1935–1941, during his composition of the other historical-autobiographical plays. It is, I think, safe to assume that it evolved considerably during that time (the letter to Sisk in 1935 is too early in the cycle's composition history to be definitive). We can say, from the evidence of his third draft, that it shares with his other late plays a concern with both his own life experience and his vision of the American experience. These themes also occur in O'Neill's other unfinished works of this period—"Blind Alley Guy," "The Visit of Malatesta," and "The Last Conquest" (at one point called "The Thirteenth Apostle"). Questions of good and evil and man's capacity for both, the seductive nature of wealth and power, the relationship of past and present, love and possession—these are the themes of all the late plays, *More Stately Mansions* included.

Chothia is right in pointing to some of its admittedly cumbersome, middle-period techniques, but the scenario of *The Calms of Capricorn* does not suggest that O'Neill contemplated using them in *Mansions'* sequel. *More Stately Mansions* may not be as stylistically typical of the cycle as she assumes. See Chothia, *Forging a Language: A Study of the Plays of Eugene O'Neill* and Manheim, *Eugene O'Neill's New Language of Kinship.*

4. For parallels between Deborah and Ella O'Neill and Sara and Carlotta, for instance, see Sheaffer, *Artist,* 482–83. Bogard points to the parallels between Deborah and Mary Tyrone, Simon and Edmund, and Sara and Josie (384–85). Manheim rejects the link between Joel and Jamie O'Neill, seeing Joel instead as emerging from that part of O'Neill afraid to "expose himself to an authentic human relationship" (118).

5. Sophus K. Winther, "Eugene O'Neill—The Dreamer Confronts His Dream," *Arizona Quarterly,* 21 (Autumn 1965): 232.

6. Louis Sheaffer, *O'Neill: Son and Playwright* (Boston: Little, Brown and Company, 1968) 506.

7. For a psychoanalytic treatment of Deborah as a portrayal of O'Neill's mother and the relationship between this play and *Long Day's Journey,* see Albert Rothenberg, M.D., "Autobiographical Drama: Strindberg and O'Neill," *Literature and Psychology,* 17. 2–3 (1967): 95–114. "The unfinished play *More Stately Mansions* seems to represent the raw emotions and raw material out of which *Long Day's Journey into Night* developed," Rothenberg concludes (105).

8. Frederick Wilkins posits quite rightly that O'Neill's quarrel is not with the ideals of the original Puritans or the theoretical tenets of Calvinism so much as it is with

    the distortions of those ideals after the backsliding of the seventeenth century, the ascetic and narrow emphases of the eighteenth century, and the evolution of materialism and a cold, business mentality in the eighteenth and nineteenth centuries, when men like Franklin turned the Protestant ethic of work away from its original goal, of glorifying God, to a new goal, of increasing man's material prosperity. (240)

    Although I see Franklin as more concerned with societal, political, and philanthropic concerns than with amassing a fortune, I certainly agree with the major thrust of Wilkins' thesis. In Joel Harford we see one of O'Neill's cold, businesslike, and exceedingly grim Puritans. See Wilkins, "The Pressure of Puritanism in O'Neill's New England Plays," in Virginia Floyd, ed., *Eugene O'Neill: A World View* (New York: Frederick Ungar Publishing Co., 1979) 237–44.

9. Floyd points out that Simon's cabin, ten by fifteen feet with a roof of hand-hewn shingles and overlooking a lake, duplicates exactly Thoreau's hut at Walden, described in Van Wyck Brooks'

The Flowering of New England 1815-1865, a book that O'Neill had read and made notes from. See Floyd, *At Work*, 217n.

10. It should be mentioned that while the "more stately mansions" of the title refers ironically to Oliver Wendell Holmes' sentimental and idealistic poem, "The Chambered Nautilus," it also draws upon Christ's allusion to the "many mansions" in his Father's house (John 14:2).

11. The connections between the success ideology and its Calvinistic origins are well known and require little comment. Franklin's *Autobiography* and his aphorisms in *Poor Richard* detail the ways in which the virtues of the elect can promote success in business. Conversely, the aura of salvation that characterized the saints of the New England meeting house shone around their successors, the prosperous merchants of the Exchange. The "way to wealth" was also the road to salvation. Material wealth, regarded by Puritan popularizers as a frequent, though not necessary, sign of God's favor, retained its resonance of divine approval in nineteenth-century America. Simon's desires for wealth, power, and economic self-sufficiency indicate the triumph, during this period, of the new elect, the captains of industry whose successors were to be the Vanderbilts and the Morgans, the Carnegies and the Rockefellers.

12. This development, too, is culturally derived. In nineteenth-century America, as urbanization set in and the American male became tainted by his business dealings, the woman was increasingly regarded as the locus of virtue, the pure and the undefiled priestess of hearth, home, and spirituality. Women kept the flame, not only of the hearth, but of truth, goodness, purity, and hope in the soiled urban world.

13. The spiritual underpinnings of Deborah's daydream kingdom bear a striking, if at first glance incongruous, resemblance to the Calvinist perspective that informed the Puritanism of the founding fathers. Both doctrinaire Calvinism and the theory of divine right maintain that the ruler has absolute and total power to favor whomever he chooses. Grace is conferred upon the individual by an arbitrary act of the God/King; it cannot be earned and is never merited. But when granted, the status conferred by election becomes the channel to power. Thus in her fantasies, when Deborah becomes the king's consort, she assumes his power and takes on the privileges of divine right. Her salvation (i.e., her status) is absolute. Just so, in doctrinaire Calvinism the corrupt sinner who is cleansed by God's grace and chosen to be one of the elect is the beneficiary of His grace and power.

14. Northrop Frye, *Anatomy of Criticism: Four Essays* (Princeton: Princeton University Press, 1957) 186.

15. A contrasting allusion occurs in the cluster of references to Napoleon, a man of facts and action, cf. the dreamy withdrawal associated with Byron's poetry. When Simon becomes a successful businessman, Deborah quite pointedly calls him a "Napoleon of affairs," one who is mindful of linear time, paying attention to the present and looking to the future.

16. Deborah's repetition of the Louis XIV fantasy in the opening scene reminds us of Con's Byronic incantations. It is ironic that while she interrupts and ridicules Con in *A Touch of the Poet*, Con's daughter Sara overhears *her* private reverie in the sequel play.

17. This detail, the Chinese lacquer red, is also interesting from an autobiographical standpoint, since it draws attention to the parallels between Deborah's garden and Tao House, designed and decorated by Carlotta O'Neill. The Harford garden is surrounded by a brick wall eight feet high; the O'Neills' home was also surrounded by a high concrete wall. The octagonal summer house suggests the shape of a pagoda; its door is painted a Chinese lacquer red. Carlotta chose an Oriental decor for Tao House, and all its interior doors were painted a bright Chinese

orange or red. The unnatural atmosphere of Deborah's garden seems also to have prevailed at the O'Neill mansion. In the entrance hall was a green mirror, for instance, that reportedly gave back a ghastly image, and the entire house had an inward, brooding atmosphere since Carlotta, who could not endure the sun's bright glare, kept the venetian blinds closed most of the time (see Sheaffer, *Artist,* 472).

18. Deborah's garden presents a striking contrast to Simon's office, which is adorned with pictures of Washington, Hamilton, Webster, and Calhoun. Although both settings are linked with historical precedents, the connotations are quite different. Deborah's love fantasies do not revolve around the "real" Sun King, but some generalized vision of a romantic, powerful suitor, while the portraits in Simon's office, one assumes, are there to serve as models for the rising young entrepreneur. The former looks to the past as ideal and suggests a withdrawal from the hurly-burly of everyday life; the latter is linked to the present moment and the future. The past represented by Simon's pictures is relatively recent; as an American, it is the matrix from which he emerges. The era of Louis XIV, on the other hand, is the late seventeenth and early eighteenth centuries; it represents not Deborah's actual heritage but a wish-fulfillment.

   These contrasting images, like the contrasting allusions to Byron and Napoleon, indicate the care and precision with which O'Neill crafted this play. Although it admittedly remains in rough form, having progressed only through a third draft, it contains the elements of a major work, had he been able to finish it.

19. Sara's Irish syntax has returned with her Gaelic values, reflected in her decision to return to the soil and her determination to take care of her family. When Deborah emerges from the summerhouse, totally absorbed in her dream world, it is appropriate that she takes Sara for the Irish kitchen maid—and that it is a role which Sara accepts.

Chapter 4

1. See Donald Gallup's Introductory Note in *Calms,* vii–xi, for a more detailed discussion of the history of conception and composition. Further references to this volume will be designated *Calms* and included parenthetically in the text. Also consult Bogard, 374–76 and 380–81 and Floyd, *At Work,* 215–22. Floyd identifies the dates of "The Earth is the Limit" as the 1860s, a slight variance from Bogard's figure. She also points to robber baron Jay Gould as a probable model for Jonathan Harford, and Pierpont Morgan, the autocratic banker, as at least a partial source for the character of Wolfe.

2. O'Neill wrote to Theresa Helburn and the Theater Guild in 1936 that his first drafts were "intolerably long and wordy—intentionally so, because I put everything in them, so as not to lose anything, and rely on a subsequent revision and rewriting, after a lapse of time with better perspective on them, to concentrate on the essential and eliminate the overweight." Quoted in *Calms* xii.

3. In the process of supervising a student rendering of *The Calms of Capricorn* at the University of Wisconsin at Madison in December 1981 and January 1982, Professor Esther Jackson consulted two naval experts, both of whom attested to the psychological accuracy of O'Neill's portrayal of the becalmed passengers, citing personal knowledge of strange aberrations of behavior that have occurred under similar conditions.

4. It is perhaps worth noting that the name of Ethan's clipper ship, *Dream of the West,* insofar as I have been able to ascertain, is fictitious; that of the *Flying Cloud,* whose record he attempts to beat, is historical. Designed and built by the famous Donald McKay of Boston, the *Flying Cloud's* first captain was a New Englander named Josiah P. Creesy. On her maiden voyage in 1851, Creesy and his navigator wife completed the New York to San Francisco voyage in a stunning eighty-nine days and twenty-one hours, beating the previous ninety-six-day record

of the *Surprise* by nearly a week. When, after completing her around-the-world voyage, the *Flying Cloud* sailed into New York harbor, she was greeted with a riotous welcome; the newspapers hailed the voyage as a national triumph. For further background information, see A. B. C. Whipple's *The Clipper Ships* (Alexandria, Virginia: Time-Life Books, 1980). Floyd (*At Work*, 216) identifies O'Neill's sources as Richard McKay, *Some Famous Sailing Ships and Their Builder Donald McKay* (New York, 1931) and Arthur H. Clark, *The Clipper Ship Era* (Riverside, Connecticut, 1910).

5. A financial panic was precipitated on August 24, 1857, by the failure of the New York City branch of the Ohio Life Insurance Company, caused primarily by over-speculation in railway securities and real estate. 4,932 businesses failed that year; by 1859, another eight thousand went under. See Gorton Garruth and Associates, eds., *Encyclopedia of American Facts and Dates*, 6th edition (New York: Thomas Y. Crowell Company, 1972) 252.

6. Arthur Miller uses a similar technique in *Death of a Salesman*, with Biff and Hap representing the two primary thrusts of Willy's personality. Hap vows to make his mark in the business world, while Biff is the agrarian, happy out-of-doors and "good with his hands."

Chapter 5

1. Eugene O'Neill, *The Iceman Cometh* (New York: Random House, 1940) 25. All future quotations will be taken from this edition, with page numbers included parenthetically in the text.

2. Earlier, that is, in terms of their conception and initial drafts, not necessarily their dates of completion. O'Neill continued to revise *Poet* up until 1942 and never finished *More Stately Mansions*.

3. For the most concise and thorough information on the autobiographical sources for the characters in *Iceman*, see Floyd, *At Work*, 260-68. With the possible exception of McGloin and the tarts, all the characters seem to be based partially or wholly on people O'Neill knew or knew of; interestingly, O'Neill says that "the most imaginary character in the play" is Hickey (Sheaffer, *Artist*, 498).

4. See Laurin R. Porter, "*The Iceman Cometh* as Crossroad in O'Neill's Long Journey," *Modern Drama*, 31 (March 1988): 56-62.

5. That was the winter of O'Neill's attempted suicide at Jimmy-the-Priest's, a New York waterfront dive where he had been living with the bums and outcasts he later immemorialized in *The Iceman Cometh*. That same summer saw him living with his family in a rare period of relative harmony at the New London Monte Cristo cottage; shortly thereafter he learned of his consumption and left for the sanitorium, where he made his famous resolution to become a playwright. Thus, both personally and artistically, O'Neill's life turned around that year; *Iceman* and *Long Day's Journey* tell the story of his two "families" at that critical juncture.

6. Sullivan's prototype is suggested in Joe Mott's interview with "de Big Chief." Although Harry refers to the chief as "Big Bill," it is likely that O'Neill's model was "Big Tim" Sullivan. For the most thorough analysis of the cultural milieu of *Iceman*, see John Henry Raleigh's *The Plays of Eugene O'Neill* (Carbondale: Southern Illinois University Press, 1965) 66-75.

7. A frequently quoted anecdote has it that when Laurence Langner suggested that O'Neill eliminate some of the references to "pipe dreams," noting that the phrase or its equivalent was expressed eighteen times, the playwright replied emphatically, "I *intended* it to have been repeated eighteen times!" (see, e.g., Sheaffer, *Artist*, 572).

8. Egil Tornqvist, *A Drama of Souls: Studies in O'Neill's Supernaturalistic Technique* (New Haven: Yale University Press, 1969) 249-50.

9. An interesting detail in this regard is the fact that Mosher has a heavy brass watch-chain but no watch (*Iceman* 7).

10. The communion motif has received its fullest treatment in Cyrus Day's classic article, "The Iceman and the Bridegroom," in which he points out the parallels between Leonardo da Vinci's painting of the last supper and O'Neill's careful staging of Harry's birthday party. Like Christ, Day points out, Hickey has twelve disciples. They all drink wine at the party, and Hickey leaves, again like Christ, aware that he goes to his execution. The three tarts correspond with the three Marys, while

> one of the derelicts, Parritt, resembles Judas Iscariot in several ways. He is the twelfth in the list of dramatis personae; Judas is twelfth disciple in the New Testament. He has betrayed his anarchist mother for a paltry $200; Judas betrayed Christ for thirty pieces of silver. He is from the far-away Pacific Coast; Judas was from far-away Judaea. Hickey reads his mind and motives; Christ reads Judas's. Parritt compares himself to Iscariot when he says that his mother would regard anyone who quit the "Movement" as a Judas who ought to be boiled in oil. He commits suicide by jumping off a fire escape; Judas fell from a high place (Acts 1:18) or "hanged himself" (Matthew 27:5).

See Cyrus Day, "The Iceman and the Bridegroom," *Modern Drama*, 1 (May 1958): 6–7.

11. Of the many commentators who point to the confessional elements of *Iceman*, Raleigh provides the most thorough history of the background and practice of confession, as well as its occurrence in Western literature. He distinguishes between two types: the private (auricular) confession made to a priest and the public one made to the community at large. Parritt's confession to Larry is of the former variety; Hickey's to Hope and the boarders, the latter. John Henry Raleigh, "The Last Confession: O'Neill and the Catholic Confessional," in Floyd, *World View*, 212–28.

12. The proprietor of Jimmy-the-Priest's, the model for Hope, "earned his name because he looked more like an ascetic than a saloonkeeper" (see Gelbs 161–62). To the extent that Harry partakes of this role, he parallels Slade not just as patriarch but also as father-confessor.

13. The confessional experience brings Parritt relief not because it cancels his sin, but because it allows him his punishment (note Slade's "God damn you" as he sends him to his death). If the ritual were fully efficacious, both penitents would be reincorporated into the community, but this is not the case. Hickey and Parritt remain intruders to the end.

14. Leonard Chabrowe, in *Ritual and Pathos: The Theater of O'Neill* (Lewisburg, Pa.: Bucknell University Press, 1976) sees O'Neill's aesthetics in terms of two primary thrusts: the theater as a temple to Dionysus and drama as a ritualistic celebration of life, on the one hand, and the idea of life as inevitably tragic on the other. The former culminates for Chabrowe in *The Iceman Cometh;* the latter, in *Long Day's Journey*. Of *Iceman* he writes, "Life, with its manifold suffering, is accepted and renewed through a celebratory experience of it. For a celebratory experience, a participation in ritual, a singing and dancing about life, exorcises all pain and the fear of death, magically invoking more life" (97–98). I have difficulty reconciling the play's decidedly bleak conclusion about the necessity of illusions and life as a waiting for death with Chabrowe's notion of a "celebratory experience." One hardly experiences *Iceman* as "magically invoking more life."

15. For a more detailed treatment of this matter, see my "*Hughie*: Pipe Dream for Two" in James J. Martine, ed., *Critical Essays on Eugene O'Neill* (Boston: G. K. Hall, 1984) 178–88.

16. The following February, O'Neill refers in his notes to what may have been a ninth play in the series, the "Thompson-rat idea." See Floyd, *At Work*, 346n.

17. See Floyd, *At Work*, 349.

18. Gelbs, 844.

19. Eugene O'Neill, *Hughie* (New Haven: Yale University Press, 1959) 7. Subsequent citations in the text refer to this edition and will be indicated parenthetically.

20. Smith also resembles Hickey in that he is associated with chronological time in the play. If Hickey prides himself on never forgetting a face, Erie is a whiz at guessing ages. He accurately puts Charlie at forty-three or forty-four, though he looks over fifty; the clerk himself can't remember which it is.

21. Henry Hewes, "*Hughie,*" *Saturday Review*, October 4, 1958; rpt. Oscar Cargill, N. Bryllion Fagin, William J. Fisher, eds., *O'Neill and His Plays: Four Decades of Criticism* (New York: New York University Press, 1961) 226.

22. Bogard notes in this regard:

    > The use of the key is important stage business. It is the only non-verbal sound from within the lobby until the dice roll along the counter at the end of the play. O'Neill marks the turning point in the play, the moment when Erie hits the farthest ebb of his loneliness, with the stage direction, "*For a while he is too defeated even to twirl his room key*" (*Hughie* 30). The moment was underscored memorably in the Stockholm production when the actor, Bengt Eklund, dropped the key. In so bare a scene, the action, the loss of the fetish, assumed climactic proportions. (Bogard 420n)

23. There are those who disagree with me on this point. Raleigh, in *The Plays of Eugene O'Neill*, calls *Hughie* "one of the most optimistic plays that O'Neill ever wrote" (28). J. Dennis Rich also takes this position. Rich sees the late plays (*Iceman, Long Day's Journey*, and *Hughie*) as existential in their vision, dramatizing Camus's definition of the absurd: man's confrontation with a meaningless universe. See "Exile without Remedy: The Late Plays of Eugene O'Neill," in Floyd, *World View*, 257–76.

Chapter 6

1. Sheaffer, *Playwright*, 240.

2. For information on the composition history of *Long Day's Journey* see Floyd, *At Work*, 281–97 and Judith E. Barlow, "*Long Day's Journey into Night*: From Early Notes to Finished Play," *Modern Drama*, 22 (March 1979): 19–28. Barlow's article traces the changes in characterization of each of the four Tyrones through successive drafts. In each case the final treatment is more sympathetic than the original one; "the act of composition apparently was, for O'Neill, a lesson in compassion," she concludes (19). For further detail, see chapter 2 of Barlow's *Final Acts: The Creation of Three Late O'Neill Plays* (Athens: The University of Georgia Press, 1985).

3. For a psychoanalytic analysis of the Tyrones' interactional patterns, see Stephen A. Black, "The War Among the Tyrones," *The Eugene O'Neill Newsletter*, 11 (Summer–Fall 1987): 29–31.

4. As we shall see shortly, however, this linear movement, like that of morning to night, will ultimately turn on itself and become cyclic.

5. It is an interesting biographical detail that, although most of the other elements of any importance in *Long Day's Journey* correspond with the facts of O'Neill's life as his biographers have been able to construct them, the biography does not corroborate this position. Ella O'Neill did, in fact, finally overcome her addiction in a manner symbolically similar to the one described at the end of act 2: she returned to a convent. After her stay there, she remained abstemious

until her death in 1922. It would seem that as he writes this play the critical reality for O'Neill is not the fact that his mother overcame her addiction eventually but that she was addicted at all.

6. Although Eugene's birth and its painful aftermath may have been the cause of Ella O'Neill's addiction (and there is some reason to doubt even that), his bout with consumption did not occasion her return to morphine. This suggests, perhaps, that the guilt O'Neill felt for her addiction is exaggerated out of proportion to the facts. Ironically, it may also indicate a kind of wish fulfillment. In the play, Mary clearly favors Edmund over Jamie and is so distraught over her younger son's illness that she turns to morphine to escape her pain. In real life, this does not seem to be the case. The biography suggests that Ella was actually closer to Jamie than Eugene and seemed almost indifferent to the playwright's illness—or at least, certainly not as concerned as the play suggests.

7. Robert C. Lee, "Eugene O'Neill's Remembrance: The Past is the Present," *Arizona Quarterly,* 23 (Winter 1967): 296.

8. See Sheaffer, *Playwright,* 126.

9. According to Irish folklore, the wail of a banshee foretold the impending death of a family member; a banshee, I might add, is a *female* spirit.

10. For further discussion of O'Neill's use of allusions in *Long Day's Journey,* see Chothia, 175–81.

11. This phenomenon in the play is borne out in biographical fact. James O'Neill, a first-generation immigrant, was born in Ireland; Ella, second generation, was born in America of Irish parents; and the two sons, representing still another generation, were born in the United States, of American parents.

12. Although the play is not mentioned by name, this is clearly the melodrama Mary refers to on page 105.

13. At the end of his monologue, Edmund grins wryly and says, "It was a great mistake, my being born a man, I would have been much more successful as a sea gull or a fish. As it is, I will always be a stranger who never feels at home, who does not really want and is not really wanted, who can never belong, who must always be a little in love with death!" (*LDJ* 153–54). This is as true of the playwright as it is of Edmund. O'Neill is a "stranger who never feels at home," one "always . . . a little in love with death" (hence his switching names with his dead brother in the play). The guilt which he experienced as a result of Ella's addiction could only be stilled in a transcendent mingling with the universe and concomitant abdication of identity or in the ultimate loss of identity—death.

14. One of the reasons this play speaks so movingly to American audiences is that, like the Tyrones, we experience a vague, nameless guilt associated with a lost ideal. The American dream stems from a collective vision of a past in which all opposites were reconciled; in the moment that informs this ideal, individualism and brotherhood, spiritual and material wealth, progress and traditionalism coexisted in some miraculous fashion. This "radical innocence," to quote Ihab Hassan, is a "property of the mythic American Self" and explains why, according to psychologists and cultural analysts like Rollo May, America is such a nation of self-haters: a disjuncture between the dream and the reality is inevitable from the moment it enters the stream of history. As a tale of lost innocence, then, *Long Day's Journey into Night* recapitulates a major motif in the American experience (see Ihab Hassan, *Radical Innocence: Studies in the Contemporary American Novel* [Princeton: Princeton University Press, 1961] 6).

15. What I call "accusational cycles" is similar to Manheim's "language of kinship."

16. This same pattern of accusation-retraction is found in O'Neill's personal letters. The following example is taken from a letter written to Agnes Boulton shortly after he left her for Carlotta

Monterey: "And won't you be just too tickled to death to feel that you can—for the present, anyway—hurt my work! A grand revenge! But maybe I wrong you. If so, I apologize" (Sheaffer, *Artist*, 298).

17. Eugene O'Neill, *Mourning Becomes Electra* (New York: Horace Liveright, Inc., 1931) 256.

18. Jamie's account of his discovery of Mary's addiction points to this thematic connection; "I'd never dreamed before that any women but whores took dope!" he says (*LDJ* 163). This relationship is reinforced by the parallels between Mary and Fat Violet, Jamie's consort: both feel they are too fat (Mary has gained twenty pounds), both play the piano, both are lonely.

Though at first glance the identification of Mary with prostitutes seems incongruous, biographical facts further substantiate this connection. O'Neill's mother, though actually named Mary Ellen, at age fifteen dropped "Mary" for "Ellen" and after her marriage switched to the name "Ella," which from that time forward she used on all her legal documents, including her will (Gelbs 11). Although psychiatrists and critics have suggested that by calling her "Mary" in *Long Day's Journey* O'Neill intended to link his mother to the Virgin Mary, stressing symbolically her desire to renounce earthly responsibilities for loftier spiritual concerns, which is likely enough, the name "Mary Ellen" was also a slang expression for an amateur prostitute, a term with which O'Neill was familiar. By using the name Mary, the playwright reminds us that his mother's given name was not Ella, but Mary Ellen.

Chapter 7

1. Manheim 191.

2. Eugene O'Neill, *A Moon for the Misbegotten* (New York: Random House, 1974) 95. Subsequent quotations will be taken from this edition and included parenthetically in the text with the designation *Moon*.

3. Phil Hogan's three sons, by representing various levels of assimilation into the American culture, serve to emphasize Phil and Josie's ethnicity. The play begins with Mike Hogan, "a New England Irish-Catholic Puritan, Grade B," leaving the farm to make his way in the world. Like his two brothers before him, he has absorbed the American ambition to "get ahead" and thus prepares to leave his rural existence for the opportunities awaiting in the city. A decidedly self-righteous teetotaler, he takes after Josie's mother's family, "a pious lousy lot . . . too busy preaching temperance to have time for a drink" (*Moon* 11). Mike and another son, John, now a barkeeper in Meriden, comprise the antithetical Irish attitude toward drinking. Thomas, the third brother, is "way up in the world, a noble sergeant of the Bridgeport police," as Josie says sarcastically (*Moon* 3). Though they retain Irish traits, the Hogan boys are quickly absorbed into the American mainstream. They have put their past behind them; "they've not written me in years," Josie complains (*Moon* 5).

4. It is interesting in this regard that at one time O'Neill was considering the title "The Moon Bore Twins" for this play.

5. The Gelbs' description of Jamie and Ella O'Neill's relationship after James' death confirms the play's depiction of Tyrone's total devotion to his mother:

> Ella and Jamie, completely dependent upon each other since James' death, always dined together at restaurants and attended the theatre together—including the premières of *The Emperor Jones*, *Diff'rent*, *Anna Christie*, *Gold* and *The Straw*. Jamie had not touched any liquor since making his vow and, to friends who saw him during that period he seemed relaxed, gentle and happy, perhaps for the first time in his life. (491)

6. It is important to recall that for most of acts 2 and 3, it seems to Josie as well as to the audience that Tyrone has reneged on his bargain. In agreeing to accept Harder's lucrative offer for the Hogan farm, as Josie sees it, Tyrone has not only betrayed his Irish blood; he has joined forces with the enemy and become the hated English landlord. This, I would argue, accounts for the considerable time which O'Neill devotes to the Harder-Hogan confrontation. Critics such as Doris Falk, who complains that too much of act 1 is wasted on the Harder episode, do not appreciate what O'Neill is doing here. Not only is he setting up the Irish-Yankee conflict, a central tension in the play; he is also painting a portrait of what Jim could become.

7. See footnote 18, chapter 6.

8. The lyrics of "Mother Macree," by Rida Johnson Young, are as follows:

> There's a spot in me heart which no coleen may own,
> There's a depth in me soul never sounded or known;
> There's a place in my mem'ry, my life that you fill,
> No other can take it, no one ever will.
> Sure I love the dear silver that shines in your hair.
> And the brow that's all furrowed, and wrinkled with care.
> I kiss the dear fingers, so toil-worn for me.
> O, God bless you and keep you, Mother Macree!
>
> Ev'ry sorrow or care in the dear days gone by,
> Was made bright by the light of the smile in your eye:
> Like a candle that's set in a window at night
> Your fond love has cheered me, and guided me right.

(M. Witmark & Sons, 1910. Music by Chauncey Olcott and Ernest R. Ball)

9. It is perhaps worth noting that the religious dimensions of the play—"Jim Tyrone's attempt to find forgiveness, through his confession to Josie, and redemption"—were not added until the final, 1943 draft. Floyd suggests that O'Neill was motivated by personal as well as artistic considerations here. His health rapidly deteriorating in these final months of his writing career, he experienced a sincere desire to be reconciled with a brother he deeply loved as well as his own need for a benediction (*At Work*, 382–83). This dovetails nicely with her reading of Josie as O'Neill's alter-ego, since both are blessed by this moment of moonlight grace.

10. O'Neill once commented, "In all my plays sin is punished and redemption takes place"—as precise a summary of *A Moon* as one could hope for (Croswell Bowen, *The Curse of the Misbegotten*, [London: Rupert Hart-Davis, 1960] 309).

11. The resurrection theme is reinforced by two of Tyrone's Shakespearean allusions. "Hark, Hark, the Donnegal lark" (*Moon* 68) is an allusion to Cloten's morning serenade to Imogen in *Cymbeline* ("Hark, Hark! the lark at heaven's gate sings, / And Phoebus 'gins arise"). The sunshiney morning of Shakespeare's song and the poem's conclusion, which bids Imogen arise, reflect the resurrection motif of *A Moon for the Misbegotten*'s final act. *Cymbeline*, of course, is a resurrection play. Not only do Imogen and Posthumus, both thought dead, appear magically in the closing scenes; so do Cymbeline's two long-lost sons. As in *A Moon*, the family is reunited in the play's final scene.

"It is the very error of the moon" (*Moon* 99) is said by Othello, thinking he has killed Desdemona. She is not yet dead, however; Shakespeare resurrects her long enough to say, "Commend me to my kind lord." Othello is reunited with her in death.

(It is one of the quirks of fate that the 1973 revival of *A Moon for the Misbegotten*, which director Jose Quintero called the Resurrection Company, "resurrected not only Quintero's career and those of the two stars, Jason Robards and Colleen Dewhurst, but the reputation of O'Neill, once and for all'' [*Moon* vi].)

12. Raleigh points out that "women in one phase of Irish mythology were assigned an especially significant role" as "the spiritual vehicle who conveys the soul of the dead to rebirth in a later generation" ("The Irish Atavism of *A Moon*," in Floyd, *World View*, 234–35). Though he sees Josie's efforts as futile in this regard, I would want to argue that spiritually, if not physically, Jim experiences a rebirth through her ministrations.

13. In the character of Jim Tyrone the playwright incorporates characteristics of James O'Neill as they appear in the portrait of James Tyrone in *Long Day's Journey*. In the first instance, he is now called "Tyrone," the name assigned to James in the previous play. Like James Tyrone, Jim is a frequent patron of the inn, where he often buys drinks for the house—a far cry from the young Jamie in *Long Day's Journey*. He has taken over James' role as landlord and derives the same pleasure in real estate negotiations, as evidenced by his dealings with Harder's superintendent, Simpson.

    He has even adopted the elder Tyrone's rhetoric—for instance, the use of the word "poison" to describe the effects of his alcoholic bitterness. In *Long Day's Journey* James warns Edmund that Jamie will "poison" his life; in *A Moon* Jim himself warns Josie, "I'd poison it for myself and for you." (Excluding references to poison ivy in connection with the Harker/Harder episode, the words "poison" or "poisoned" occur eleven times in *Long Day's Journey*, seven times in *A Moon for the Misbegotten*. The first eleven occurrences are James'; the last seven are Jamie's.) As before, Jamie is given to quoting Shakespeare. But where he quotes Iago in *Long Day's Journey* he now quotes Othello, one of James O'Neill's favorite Shakespearean characters.

    Other allusions also underline the difference between the Jamie of *Long Day's Journey* and the Jim Tyrone of *A Moon*. In the earlier play Jamie's range of quotations is limited to the Decadents and sarcastic quips from Kipling and Shakespeare; the Jim Tyrone of *A Moon for the Misbegotten* is more mellow. Although two of his three Shakespearean allusions are used mockingly ("Hark, Hark, the Donnegal lark," 69, and "It is the very error of the moon," 99), the venom has disappeared from his voice. He is still cynical; he quotes Rossetti and Dowson's "Cynara." But whereas in *Long Day's Journey* Edmund recites the Dowson poem as he envisions Jamie ironically quoting it to some "poor fat burlesque queen [who] doesn't get a word of it" (*LDJ* 134), in *A Moon* Tyrone repeats the phrase sincerely to Josie: "I love you a lot—in my fashion" (*Moon* 77). The absence of quotation marks indicates that he has integrated the poem's emotion into his own life; it is no longer ironic—though in a cynical moment he later tries to shrug it off. In addition the overall number of references to the Decadents decreases (there are no allusions to Wilde or Swinburne, for example, as in *Long Day's Journey*); Tyrone now quotes Keats and Virgil instead—the kind of poet likely to be found in James Tyrone's library.

    It is not necessary, of course, to look either to the biography or to *Long Day's Journey* for evidence of Jamie's identification with his father; O'Neill has provided ample evidence of this phenomenon in the play itself. His ritualistic wrangling with Phil Hogan, for example, is a repetition of a pattern established years earlier by James Tyrone. Even his relationship with Josie is anticipated in the story she tells about James' coming to collect overdue rent when Phil would send her out to soften him up.

    Still another layer of the character suggests that the Tyrone of *A Moon for the Misbegotten* represents not only James and Jamie, but also Edmund (hence, the assignation of the family name.) The biographical data reveals, for instance, that many of the opinions attributed to Jim in *A Moon* are actually those of the playwright himself. The association of sex with whores as well as the identification of prostitutes with mother figures is also typical of O'Neill and a frequent motif in his plays.

    Thus in his final drama, O'Neill resurrects his entire family, including Mary, who is present in the form of Josie Hogan.

14. "The Praties They Grow Small" is an Irish song which probably dates back to the great potato famine which precipitated the waves of Irish immigration to America around the middle of the nineteenth century. As such, it recalls the immigrant background of both Ella and James O'Neill, whose parents were among the thousands to seek relief from the famine in the United States.
The theme of diminishment reflected in the verse Phil Hogan sings is picked up again in verse 3:

> Oh we're trampled in the dust,
> Over here, over here,
> Oh we're trampled in the dust,
> But the lord in whom we trust
> Will give us crumb for crust,
> Over here, over here.

The "over here," of course, where the potatoes grow smaller and "we're trampled in the dust," is America ("The Praties They Grow Small," *A Collection of 20 Songs and Ballads,* ed. Richard Dyer-Bennett [Radio City, New York: Leeds Music Corporation, 1946], 33–34).

Chapter 8

1. Bogard, 384.

2. See Manheim for an explanation of similar relationship patterns in these plays as revealed in the love-hate "language of kinship."

Selected Bibliography

Alexander, Doris. *The Tempering of Eugene O'Neill.* New York: Harcourt, Brace and World, 1962.

Altizer, Thomas J. J. "Eternal Recurrence and Kingdom of God." *The New Nietzsche.* Ed. David B. Allison. Cambridge, Mass.: The MIT Press, 1985.

Barlow, Judith E. *Final Acts: The Creation of Three Late O'Neill Plays.* Athens: University of Georgia Press, 1985.

_____. "*Long Day's Journey into Night*: From Early Notes to Finished Play." *Modern Drama,* 22 (March 1979): 19-28.

Black, Stephen A. "The War Among the Tyrones." *The Eugene O'Neill Newsletter* 11 (Summer-Fall 1987): 29-31.

Bogard, Travis. *Contour in Time: The Plays of Eugene O'Neill.* New York: Oxford University Press, 1972.

Boulton, Agnes. *Part of a Long Story.* Garden City: Doubleday, 1958.

Bowen, Croswell. "The Black Irishman." *PM,* November 3, 1946. Rpt. in *O'Neill and His Plays: Four Decades of Criticism.* Eds. Oscar Cargill, N. Bryllion Fagin, William J. Fisher. New York: New York University Press, 1961. 64-84.

_____. *Curse of the Misbegotten: A Tale of the House of O'Neill.* London: Rupert Hart-Davis, 1960.

Cargill, Oscar, N. Bryllion Fagin, and William J. Fisher, eds. *O'Neill and His Plays: Four Decades of Criticism.* New York: New York University Press, 1961.

Carpenter, Frederic I. *Eugene O'Neill.* New York: Twayne Publishers, 1979.

Chabrowe, Leonard. *Ritual and Pathos: The Theater of O'Neill.* Lewisburg: Bucknell University Press, 1976; London: Associated University Presses, 1976.

Chothia, Jean. *Forging a Language: A Study of the Plays of Eugene O'Neill.* Cambridge, Eng.: Cambridge University Press, 1979.

Clark, Barrett H. *Eugene O'Neill.* New York: Robert M. McBride, 1927.

_____. *Eugene O'Neill: The Man and His Plays.* New York: Dover Publications, 1947.

Day, Cyrus. "The Iceman and the Bridegroom." *Modern Drama* 1 (May 1958): 3-9.

Driver, Tom F. "On the Late Plays of Eugene O'Neill." *Tulane Drama Review* 3, No. 2 (December 1958). Rpt. in *O'Neill: A Collection of Critical Essays.* Ed. John Gassner. Englewood Cliffs, N.J.: Prentice-Hall, 1964. 110-23.

Eliade, Mircea. *The Myth of the Eternal Return.* Trans. Willard R. Trask. New York: Pantheon Books, 1954.

_____. *Myth and Reality.* Trans. Willard R. Trask. New York: Harper and Row, 1963.

Engel, Edwin A. *The Haunted Heroes of Eugene O'Neill.* Cambridge, Mass.: Harvard University Press, 1953.

Falk, Doris V. *Eugene O'Neill and the Tragic Tension: An Interpretive Study of the Plays.* New Brunswick, N.J.: Rutgers University Press, 1958.

Fay, Gerard. *The Abbey Theatre: Cradle of Genius.* Dublin: Clonmore and Reynolds, 1958.

Fitzgerald, F. Scott. *The Great Gatsby.* New York: Charles Scribner's Sons, 1925.

Fitzgerald, Geraldine. "Another Neurotic Electra: A New Look at Mary Tyrone." *Eugene O'Neill: A World View.* Ed. Virginia Floyd. New York: Frederick Ungar, 1979. 290–92.

Fitzgerald, John J. "The Bitter Harvest of O'Neill's Projected Cycle." *The New England Quarterly* 40 (September 1967): 364–74.

Floyd, Virginia, ed. *Eugene O'Neill at Work: Newly Released Ideas for Plays.* New York: Frederick Ungar, 1981.

_____, ed. *Eugene O'Neill: A World View.* New York: Frederick Ungar, 1979.

Frazer, Winifred L. *E. G. and E. G. O.: Emma Goldman and The Iceman Cometh.* Gainesville: University Presses of Florida, 1974.

Frenz, Horst. *Eugene O'Neill.* New York: Frederick Ungar, 1971.

Frye, Northrop. *Anatomy of Criticism: Four Essays.* Princeton: Princeton University Press, 1957.

Gallup, Donald, ed. *Eugene O'Neill: Work Diary* (1924–1943). 2 vols. New Haven, Conn.: Yale University Library, 1981.

Garruth, Gorton, and Associates, eds. *Encyclopedia of American Facts and Dates.* 6th edition. New York: Thomas Y. Crowell, 1972.

Gassner, John. *Eugene O'Neill.* Minneapolis: University of Minnesota Press, 1965.

_____. "Homage to O'Neill." *Theatre Time* (Summer 1951). Rpt. in *O'Neill and His Plays: Four Decades of Criticism.* Eds. Cargill et al. 321–30.

_____, ed. *O'Neill: A Collection of Critical Essays.* Englewood Cliffs, N.J.: Prentice-Hall, 1964.

Gelb, Arthur and Barbara. *O'Neill.* New York: Harper and Brothers, 1962.

Hassan, Ihab. *Radical Innocence: Studies in the Contemporary American Novel.* Princeton: Princeton University Press, 1961.

Jackson, Esther M. "O'Neill the Humanist." *Eugene O'Neill: A World View,* Ed. Virginia Floyd. New York: Frederick Ungar, 1979. 252–56.

Josephson, Lennart. *A Role: O'Neill's Cornelius Melody.* Stockholm, Sweden: Almqvist and Wiksell International, 1977; Atlantic Highlands, N.J.: Humanities Press, 1978.

Lee, Robert C. "Eugene O'Neill's Remembrance: The Past is the Present." *Arizona Quarterly* 23 (Winter 1967): 293–305.

Malone, Andrew E. "Eugene O'Neill's Limitations." *Dublin Magazine,* December 1923. Rpt. in *O'Neill and His Plays: Four Decades of Criticism.* Eds. Cargill et al. 256–65.

_____. *The Irish Drama.* New York: Benjamin Blom, 1929.

Manheim, Michael. *Eugene O'Neill's New Language of Kinship.* Syracuse: Syracuse University Press, 1982.

Miller, Jordan Y. *Eugene O'Neill and the American Critic: A Summary and Bibliographical Checklist.* 2d ed. Hamden, Conn.: Archon Books, 1973.

_____, ed. *Playwright's Progress: O'Neill and the Critics.* Chicago: Scott, Foresman, 1965.

Nietzsche, Friedrich. *Thus Spake Zarathustra.* Trans. Thomas Common. New York: The Modern Library, n.d.

O'Neill, Eugene. *The Calms of Capricorn.* Ed. Donald Gallup. New Haven and New York: Ticknor and Fields, 1982.

_____. *Hughie.* New Haven, Conn.: Yale University Press, 1959.

_____. *The Iceman Cometh.* New York: Random House, 1940.

_____. *Long Day's Journey into Night.* New Haven, Conn.: Yale University Press, 1955.

_____. *A Moon for the Misbegotten.* New York: Random House, 1974.

_____. *More Stately Mansions.* New Haven, Conn.: Yale University Press, 1964.

_____. *Mourning Becomes Electra.* New York: Horace Liveright, 1931.

_____. *A Touch of the Poet.* New Haven, Conn.: Yale University Press, 1957.

Peck, Seymour. "A Talk With Mrs. O'Neill." *The New York Times,* November 4, 1956. Rpt. in *O'Neill and His Plays: Four Decades of Criticism.* Eds. Cargill et al. 92–95.

Porter, Laurin R. "*Hughie*: Pipe Dream for Two." *Critical Essays on Eugene O'Neill.* Ed. James J. Martine. Boston: G. K. Hall, 1984. 178–88.

_____. "*The Iceman Cometh* as Crossroad in O'Neill's Long Journey." *Modern Drama* 31 (March 1988): 52–62.

Porter, Thomas E. *Myth and Modern American Drama.* Detroit: Wayne State University Press, 1969.

Potter, George. *To the Golden Door: The Story of the Irish in Ireland and America.* Boston: Little, Brown, 1960.

Raleigh, John Henry. "Eugene O'Neill and the Escape from the Chateau d'If." *O'Neill: A Collection of Critical Essays.* Ed. John Gassner. Englewood Cliffs, N.J.: Prentice-Hall, 1964. 7–22.

_____. "The Irish Atavism of *A Moon for the Misbegotten.*" *Eugene O'Neill: A World View.* Ed. Virginia Floyd. New York: Frederick Ungar, 1979. 229–36.

_____. "The Last Confession: O'Neill and the Catholic Confessional." *Eugene O'Neill: A World View.* Ed. Virginia Floyd. New York: Frederick Ungar, 1979. 212–28.

_____. "O'Neill's *Long Day's Journey into Night* and New England Irish-Catholicism." *The Partisan Review* 26 (Fall 1959). Rpt. in *O'Neill: A Collection of Critical Essays.* Ed. Gassner. 124–41.

_____. *The Plays of Eugene O'Neill.* Carbondale, Ill.: Southern Illinois University Press, 1965.

Rich, J. Dennis. "Exile Without Remedy: The Late Plays of Eugene O'Neill." *Eugene O'Neill: A World View.* Ed. Virginia Floyd. New York: Frederick Ungar, 1979. 257–76.

Rothenberg, Albert, M.D. "Autobiographical Drama: Strindberg and O'Neill." *Literature and Psychology* 17.2–3 (1967): 95–114.

_____ and Eugene D. Shapiro. "The Defense of Psychoanalysis in Literature: *Long Day's Journey into Night* and *A View from the Bridge.*" *Comparative Drama* 7 (Spring 1973): 51–67.

Roy, Emil. "The Archetypal Unity of Eugene O'Neill's Drama." *Comparative Drama* 3 (Winter 1969–70): 263–74.

Shannon, William V. *The American Irish.* New York: Macmillan, 1963.

Sheaffer, Louis. *O'Neill: Son and Artist.* Boston: Little, Brown, 1973.

_____. *O'Neill: Son and Playwright.* Boston: Little, Brown, 1968.

Skinner, Richard Dana. *Eugene O'Neill: A Poet's Quest.* New York: Longmans, Green, 1935.

Tiusanen, Timo. *O'Neill's Scenic Images.* Princeton: Princeton University Press, 1968.

Tornqvist, Egil. *A Drama of Souls: Studies in O'Neill's Supernaturalistic Technique.* New Haven, Conn.: Yale University Press, 1969.

Weissman, Philip. *Creativity in the Theater.* New York: Basic Books, 1965.

Whipple, A. B. C. *The Clipper Ships.* Alexandria, Va.: Time-Life Books, 1980.

Wilkins, Frederick. "The Pressure of Puritanism in O'Neill's New England Plays." *Eugene O'Neill: A World View.* Ed. Virginia Floyd. New York: Frederick Ungar, 1979. 237–44.

Winther, Sophus Keith. *Eugene O'Neill: A Critical Study.* New York: Russell and Russell, 1961.

_____. "Eugene O'Neill: The Dreamer Confronts His Dream." *Arizona Quarterly* 21 (Autumn 1965): 221–33.

_____. "O'Neill's Tragic Themes: *Long Day's Journey into Night.*" *Arizona Quarterly* 13 (Autumn 1957): 295–307.

Wittke, Carl. *The Irish in America.* New York: Teachers College Press, 1956.

Index